how to help the
children
survive the
divorce

how to help the
children
survive the
divorce

Alan Bradley

PhD Consultant Clinical Psychologist

& Jody Beveridge

MA Barrister at Law

foulsham

LONDON • NEW YORK • TORONTO • SYDNEY

foulsham

The Publishing House, Bennetts Close, Cippenham,
Slough, Berkshire, SL1 5AP, England

ISBN 0-572-02956-X

Cover photographs © Powerstock

A CIP record for this book is available from the British Library

While every effort has been made to ensure
the accuracy of all the information contained
within this book, neither the author nor the
publisher can be liable for any errors. In
particular, since laws change from time to
time, it is vital that each individual checks
relevant legal details for themselves.

Printed in Great Britain by Creative Print & Design (Wales), Ebbw Vale

Contents

Introduction   7

Part One: The Process of Divorce   11

Chapter 1   The Process of Change   13

Chapter 2   Family Breakdown and its Impact
on Family Members   21

Chapter 3   The Split   35

Chapter 4   Moving On   51

Chapter 5   Changing Lifestyles, Changing Roles   67

Chapter 6   New Families   79

Chapter 7   Answers to Questions Often Asked by Parents   91

Part Two: The Legal Aspects   115

Chapter 8   When Does the Law Become Involved?   117

Chapter 9   Family Mediation   123

Chapter 10   Residence and Contact Issues   127

Chapter 11   Claiming Child Support   145

Useful Contacts   149

Index   153

Introduction

Although we all enter into significant relationships with high hopes and optimism, the reality is that, at the present time, almost half of marriages end in divorce, many of which involve children. If you are thinking about – or already in the process of – separation or divorce, you will have a thousand different things on your mind: How will I survive financially? Where will I live? How long will it all take? Will I have to go to Court? Will I be okay on my own? While the issues that are important to you won't necessarily be the same as for anyone else, if you have children one of your major concerns will be how they will cope with the separation.

In writing this book, neither of us would pretend that divorce is ever easy; in fact, we have both been through the divorce process ourselves, so we each have personal experience of the issues involved. However, it should be remembered that most people – both adults and children – survive divorce or relationship breakdowns. They will, of course, be affected by their experiences, and the information in this book can help to make those experiences as painless as possible, and therefore make the outcome more positive.

> Recognising that almost all issues in divorce and separation could apply to either parent, for much of the time we have avoided using gender distinctions in the text of this book. On other occasions, particularly when covering things children say, we have referred to 'the father', 'the wife', 'mum', 'he' or 'she' etc. This is not intended in any way to be sexist but has simply been done for ease of reading.

It is important to recognise that divorce or the end of a relationship is a process and not simply an event. The run up to divorce, the divorce itself and its repercussions are likely to be a very difficult, emotional and unpleasant time for all those involved. The length of time this process takes also varies considerably; it is quite common to find people going through a period of two or more years during which their emotions and life in general are in significant turmoil. While this can be a very difficult time for the adults involved – and parents themselves deserve every care and consideration possible during this delicate process – the emphasis in this book is on the repercussions of the divorce process on children.

How to Help Your Children Survive Your Divorce is not written for academics or professionals; it is designed as a hands-on, personal guide for those individuals who are not only struggling with their own complex practical and emotional issues but who are also striving to minimise any distress or damage their children may suffer during this traumatic time. Our overriding aim is to ensure that children emerge from this difficult process not only having 'survived', but also sufficiently emotionally intact to enable them to enjoy ongoing positive relationships with both parents, as well as others in their family, and that they will in the future develop loving and caring family relationships of their own.

It is clearly the case that adult relationship breakdowns that involve children is an incredibly complex subject. With this in mind, we have divided the book into two main sections, each of which deals with the topics in manageable chunks.

The first part of the book looks at how to cope with the emotional impact of divorce on both the parents and, of course, the children involved. It covers all aspects of the divorce journey, from the initial stages of breakdown, through the feelings a child might experience at the time of the actual parting, to the grieving process following the parents' divorce. It then moves on to consider the implications of change to a child's life: perhaps moving home or school, changes to family finances, or having to adapt to their parents either being alone or having new partners who may, themselves, have children.

The first part concludes by offering answers to some of the questions often asked by parents who are experiencing divorce. This section focuses on the range of issues that would be considered 'normal' or usual to experience. The bulk of this section has been written by Alan Bradley, a practising clinical psychologist with a vast experience of helping people cope with similar situations, as it focuses on the psychological impact of divorce and how to minimise problems.

In the second part of this book, we look at a series of topics covering problems that can occur when things do not go quite as smoothly as we hoped and difficulties arise that go beyond what one would consider normal or expected. This includes what happens when the law becomes involved; mediation, residence and contact issues; and child support. It also provides advice on the many agencies that offer help and support for parents in these circumstances. This section focuses on the legal aspects and has been contributed by Jody Beveridge, a practising barrister and expert in family law.

> When discussing the psychological aspects of relationship breakdown, we have not differentiated between 'divorce' and 'separation' since the emotional impact on the individuals concerned will be unaffected by whether the parents are married or are cohabiting. This is not, however, the case where legal matters are being discussed, since the treatment by the Court of the rights and responsibilities of married parents will differ from those that will apply to couples who have been living together (see pages 118–19).

Throughout the book we have included responses to many of the statements and questions that we have been faced with, in both clinical and legal practice, on many occasions. Despite the fact that each case is unique, there are many common factors and other people's experiences can often be a useful way of illustrating constructive ways to tackle these difficult and potentially painful issues.

It is worth keeping in mind some very simple advice in these difficult circumstances:

- Don't panic. Recognise that although your children are likely to be upset and sometimes even distressed by divorce, it is certainly not inevitable that this will have a long-term negative impact on them. Both parents and children do get through divorce and go on to happier and more productive times.

- It is inevitable that even the most caring parents will make errors of judgement or behaviour at times during the process of divorce but, with an open mind and a loving attitude, the vast majority of mistakes are recoverable and will not irreversibly damage themselves or their children.

- Just by buying this book you are demonstrating that you are aware of potential problems and want to do all you can to minimise them. Hopefully the information here will help you avoid problems in the first place, recognise signals that issues need to be addressed, and learn ways of dealing with difficulties that do arise.

Part One

The Process of Divorce

The first section of this book focuses on the general process of divorce and the major issues that can affect most families in 'normal' circumstances. Thinking about the issues and anticipating potential problems can help families take action to prevent them from occurring at all, making a difficult time less traumatic for both parents and, most particularly, children.

CHAPTER 1

The Process of Change

The specific circumstances of any divorce are unique to the individuals involved, but there are many common factors, and the first is that most parents are likely to be emotionally upset, or even traumatised, by the breakdown of such an important relationship. Of course, there will be parents who are very pleased indeed to be liberated from what may have been a damaging relationship. Even so, it is difficult to disentangle oneself from such an intrinsic part of one's life without undergoing some degree of emotional turmoil, and during this phase almost all parents feel at some level overwhelmed by the circumstances in which they find themselves.

As well as this significant emotional trauma, they are likely to have to maintain their normal everyday activities and still be able to undertake the day-to-day care of their children at a time when they are struggling to cope with their own feelings. This does put a lot of pressure on parents, which is why they may be less aware of the thoughts, feelings and behaviour of their children than they would normally be. This is not to lay blame, but simply to explain why children's problems can sometimes go unnoticed by even the most caring and competent of parents.

Of course, children too are traumatised by the process of divorce, which will inevitably lead to disruptions in important relationships, as well as other significant changes in their young lives. It is not unusual for children involved in a divorce to have to move home, bringing changes to their social and educational ties. At the same time, the family's financial status may be altered, which could affect other areas of their lives. In addition, how the parents conduct themselves, especially in their dealings with each other, during this very difficult phase could have a massive direct impact on everyone involved and the children in particular.

Very competent parents can suddenly become less competent when faced with such trauma. Therefore, in addition to the direct impact, the children going through the difficulty of divorce may – for a time and for perfectly understandable reasons – lose a degree of normal support from parents who up until now had provided them with very good care indeed.

It is only too obvious that, faced with all these potential difficulties, children can become very upset and distressed. Later in the book, we will discuss ways of ensuring that parents are prepared with the capabilities to provide the best possible ongoing care for their children, even through this inevitably difficult phase.

It is important to reiterate that every relationship breakdown is unique, with huge differences in individual circumstances. The ending of an abusive or otherwise controlling relationship may be recognised as a definitely positive change to some. On the other hand, many parents are shocked and disturbed when faced with a relationship breakdown that they were simply not expecting; one partner may have suddenly announced his or her intention to end a relationship that the other partner felt was good. Under these circumstances, the partner concerned is likely to experience a range of emotions, including distress, feelings of betrayal and extremes of anger. It is also entirely possible that a breakdown comes as the culmination of many years of increasing emotional distancing by both parents equally — the partnership has come to a natural end and both adults are ready and willing to move on – to the extent that only practical issues need to be resolved and emotional trauma plays little or no part.

As well as differences in these potential scenarios of divorce, of course, how individuals respond to a particular situation will differ too. It is invariably the case that some individuals are more emotionally self-sufficient than others. We each have our individual temperament and, of course, we each have our individual life experience that has shaped the person that we are at any particular time. Individuals who have always been emotionally strong and who have a history of surviving difficulties well are likely to cope better with separation and divorce than those who do not have such a robust temperament and who find emotional problems more difficult to cope with.

The age and maturity of children

These diverse responses to separation apply to the children just as they do to the parents. All children have their own temperament, personality and life experiences, which will affect how they respond to the breakdown of their parents' relationship. Their age at the time of the breakdown, from birth to adolescence and, indeed, beyond, will also be a major factor: what is important to them and what impacts on them at each stage in their lives is quite different.

While a full discussion of child development is not appropriate in a book of this kind, it is important to recognise that children go through several major phases as they grow up. Chronological age is only a very rough indication as individual children progress through these phases at different times and at different rates. Some younger children will have significant maturity and development beyond their years, which effectively places them in an older group. On the other hand, some older children may present as intellectually or emotionally less mature than average and therefore may fall into a younger category. Furthermore, a significant life change, including separation or divorce, can cause a deliberate or subconscious shift in a child's maturity in either direction. For instance, it can happen that the oldest child of the family feels the need to protect and support a distressed parent and he or she will try to take on the role of the missing parent; or a child who is disturbed by the situation may retreat to an earlier developmental stage, perceiving it as a safer time when life was less confusing. Nonetheless, these categories are useful and allow us to consider the primary needs of children in these different stages of development when they are faced with an unusual experience.

1. Infancy: from birth to two years.

2. Pre-school: from two to five years.

3. Middle childhood: from five to ten years.

4. Early adolescence: from eleven to sixteen.

These will be the broad categories we will refer to throughout this book. Individual parents know their own children better than anyone, so they will be able to identify where their own children fall in these developmental stages.

It is, of course, sometimes the case that parents decide to separate when all their children have left home, gone to university, married or otherwise 'flown the nest'. Though it is not within the scope of this book, it is worth mentioning that even adult children may be profoundly affected by their parents' separation. They may worry about how their parents will manage on their own, both at the time and as they enter old age, and if there could be an impact on their own plans and lifestyle. They are likely to be concerned about how to break the news to the separating couple's grandchildren, if any, and how their relationship with them will be altered. If the breakdown has come unexpectedly because they had never questioned their parents' commitment to each other, older children may even find themselves examining their own marriages and feeling anxious about their futures.

The grieving process

As indicated earlier, divorce is a process and not simply an event and it is useful to have some way of understanding how this process may be operating. The following simple four-stage model has been shown to be helpful in clinical practice and is often used when working with loss in general, including bereavement. Although this may seem strange at first, divorce does involve a serious loss of a very similar kind, and the process through which the participants go is, in fact, a parallel of the grieving process.

- Stage 1: accept the reality of the loss.
- Stage 2: feel the pain of the loss.
- Stage 3: disinvest in that relationship.
- Stage 4: reinvest in other relationships.

Because it is a process, individuals need to work through one stage before they are ready to move on to the next.

The grieving process in divorce

Stage I

The first stage is coming to terms with the reality that the relationship has come to an end. Accepting the reality of separation and divorce can be problematic, especially bearing in mind that your partner is clearly still around, which of course is not the case in actual bereavement. It is particularly difficult if one of the individuals in the relationship wants it to continue even though their partner has made it clear that they wish to bring the relationship to an end. It can be months or even years before some adults come to terms with and accept the fact that the relationship is over. However, no matter how slowly or how quickly an individual grasps the fact that the relationship is over, at some stage, hopefully, they will come to that understanding and can then move on to the next stage.

Stage 2

The next stage is actually feeling the pain, trauma and upset that follows realisation that the relationship has gone. Whatever the circumstances, there will be pain, as, even if the relationship was not positive by the end, it started out as a good thing. The two individuals may arrive at this stage at different times: while one is still struggling with acceptance, the other may have understood it at a very early stage and has already gone on to feel their own emotional pain or elation, depending on how they view the ending of that relationship. However, at some stage both partners will understand that the relationship is over and experience the emotional impact of that understanding. Without experiencing the pain, or the full enormity, of the loss, individuals cannot move through this grieving process on to the next stage.

Stage 3

Following this, the individual can move to the third stage of the process, that of disinvesting in that relationship. This is the stage at which the individual acknowledges that, though they may continue to have fond memories of a relationship that has been an important part of their life and will not be forgotten, nevertheless they have to withdraw the intense feelings they have about it and in a sense let go of that relationship. This can be a very quick process for some but may be a more lengthy, traumatic process for others, depending on the circumstances. For an individual who is happy to leave a relationship, clearly that decision to disinvest will have been made at a very early stage – probably before announcing their intention to divorce. On the other hand, an individual who believed they were in a loving, caring relationship, but who was presented with the knowledge that the other partner wished to it to end, may find it very difficult indeed to disinvest emotions, thoughts and feelings regarding that partner. They may even feel it is disloyal or disrespectful towards their former partner and the life they had together to attempt to lessen the emotion. However, again, everyone needs to go through this process before they can move on to the fourth stage.

Stage 4

The final stage is moving on. Although the individual may retain some feelings for the absent partner, nevertheless they have gained sufficient control of their own feelings to disinvest to a degree where they can begin reinvesting in other relationships.

How children experience the process

As complex as this is for the adults involved in this process, it is even more difficult to understand the implications for the children of the relationship, not least because, while parents can divorce each other, parents cannot divorce their children, or indeed children divorce their parents. Once a parent means being a parent forever. Other parenting figures may come and go, but dad remains dad and mum remains mum no matter what other factors come into play in a child's life.

If we begin to look at the process that the children may be going through, however, we see that the process is very similar, that it also involves many changes and can be just, if not more, difficult.

- Stage 1: they have to come to accept the fact that their parents' relationship is over.

- Stage 2: they find this painful to varying degrees.

- Stage 3: because of changing roles and living circumstances – and perhaps other factors – the child's relationship with a parent may undergo significant change such that the child has to claw back some of the emotion invested in the parent, particularly if the parent is absent.

● Stage 4: they adapt to the changed family circumstances of their life, thrive emotionally, and if necessary accept new adults into their lives who may take over, or complement, the parenting role.

This will, of course, happen in the same way that the parent goes through a similar progression. However, the stages will not necessarily be concurrent and it is most likely that a child experiencing the four processes will be out of step with the process of the grieving parent. Moreover, the ultimate aim of the adult is to disentangle from the relationship and move on to other relationships, while it is often preferable for the child to retain a very positive ongoing relationship with the absent parent. It is often this mismatch between the caring parent and the child that leads to complex difficulties, which we will revisit later in this book; at this stage we are simply flagging up that all concerned in this relationship breakdown are going through a very complex, painful and emotional experience.

CHAPTER 2

Family Breakdown and its Impact on Family Members

No individual, couple or family has an invariable and foolproof formula for resolving problems, whether emotional, financial, domestic or concerning any other matter. They deal with their difficulties in different ways at different times. On occasion, one can have a calm and rational discussion about a problem while, at other times, there can be tears, anger and tantrums. The same is true for parents who realise their relationship with their partner is deteriorating; they might deal with matters in a calm and intellectual manner, or express their distress by making a sullen withdrawal or by giving way to angry outbursts. In extreme cases they might resort to physical and/or emotional abuse of one another.

Children's awareness of family conflict

However the parents deal with matters, it is likely that the children of the family will be well aware that there are difficulties and tensions between their parents, and between their parents and themselves, from a very early stage. While they may not understand why things are 'bad', at home, or they are not able to comprehend the complex adult issues involved, children are often more aware of emotional difficulties within families than we give them credit for.

If children pick up on signs of distress in their parents, this will clearly have an impact on them. Of course, parents are well aware of this and most of the time they try to protect the children from what is going on between them. However, it is very difficult indeed to hide these difficulties from our children and by doing so we may actually be causing them further distress or, indeed, harm.

Obvious examples are children directly witnessing angry, distressing or, indeed, violent exchanges between their parents, only to be told everything is fine, there is no problem, go away, it will be okay. However, children can also pick up on much more subtle indicators that all is not well. Clinical experience would suggest that children are often aware of distress and discomfort within the family when there are abrupt silences when they appear, or when they overhear snippets of conversation, fairly low-key arguments and, perhaps most distressing of all, arguments at night when they are supposedly safely tucked up in bed.

If children are constantly told that there are no problems and everything is fine, yet their daily experience suggests to them that this is not the truth, then, clearly, their distress at the upset within the family is multiplied by the feeling that their parents are not being totally honest with them. This can cause children to internalise their distress and stop expressing their feelings. Parents can believe that a child is coping and that things are progressing as well as possible, while in reality he or she is struggling in silence.

How parents disengage

To divorce within England and Wales you need to prove one of four things: that a spouse has committed adultery and the other cannot tolerate living with him/her; that a spouse has behaved in such a manner that you cannot reasonably be expected to remain together; that you have been separated for at least two years and both consent to a divorce OR you have been separated for five years in which case your spouse's consent is not needed; or that one spouse has deserted the other for at least two years (although this is now very rare). However, the reason most people would give for divorce or separation, which in a way encapsulates all the above legal criteria, is 'irretrievable breakdown of the relationship'.

The underlying reasons for relationship breakdowns are many and varied. As noted in Chapter 1, it is often the case that only one partner has become disenchanted and is seeking to withdraw from the relationship before the other partner is aware of this. As part of this disenchantment, the parent may already be spending less time at home, may be showing less warmth and affection to their partner, and just generally beginning the process of disengagement, not only from that relationship but also from the family as it stands at that moment. It may well be that, even when that partner is at home, because of their own thoughts and feelings they may present to the rest of family, including the children, as less interested in them, less demonstrative and unusually preoccupied.

In fact, far from thoughts of disengaging from their children, a parent might well be thinking about how to maintain a relationship with the children after a separation. Whatever the truth of the matter, from the child's point of view this parent is no longer available, either emotionally or physically, simply by spending less time at home.

Of course, it will not only be the children who pick up on this. A husband or wife who is still engaged in the relationship will be aware that their partner is less loving and caring than they might have been in the past. Because of this they may be struggling with the situation and at times are upset and tearful or exhibiting overt signs of anger or resentment. As the situation develops, or indeed deteriorates, it may well be the case that these behaviours on the part of both partners become more extreme. It is clear that this is a confusing and upsetting time for the parents who may genuinely be struggling to understand themselves, their partner, and this situation. In the midst of all of this, it can be very easy for the needs of the children to get lost.

In the course of counselling, it is not at all unusual for a child presenting with a particular difficulty to mention during more general discussion that, even though they aren't supposed to know, they are aware that their parents are not getting on, or are rowing, or the atmosphere at home is bad. The level of knowledge some children have about their parents' difficulties can come as a great surprise to their parents.

How children react to family conflict

To consider the impact on the child of this unhappy background of deteriorating parental relationships, we need to take into account that to a large extent their age and stage of development will determine their reactions and behaviour.

Infancy (0–2 years)

Clearly infants cannot talk about their problems and will understand only a few, if any, of the words that are being said around them. However, an infant who is being cared for by someone who is upset or angry or whose mood is low, who lives in an environment where there are angry and aggressive noises and where siblings may have a level of awareness of the problems and are showing behaviour disturbance can obviously be affected by all of this.

In that sense, the infant is aware that there is something wrong and in turn they are unsettled and they can exhibit such behaviours as difficulty in sleeping, changes in toilet habits, and becoming more clingy.

Preschool child (2–5 years)

As above, but by now they have a degree of understanding of the words being used.

Children at this stage tend to view the world as revolving around themselves and therefore think in terms of 'It's me you don't love' and 'It's all my fault'.

Particularly in this age group, but also in others, there can also be a tendency for children to revert to behaving in a younger way than usual. There may be a recurrence of bedwetting, difficulty separating from parent or home for any reason, unwillingness to attend nursery, and expressions of emotionality including upset.

Middle childhood (5–10 years)

Building on from above, by this age children are much more articulate and are beginning to develop a more subtle understanding of relationships and their difficulties.

Children of this age also have a wider understanding of the complexity of adult relationships. They may have some awareness of friends, neighbours or school friends who live in families where parents have split up or divorced.

On a more positive note, children of this age can begin to understand that change can be for the better, not always for the worse. It is also possible at this age for parents to engage their children in some discussions at the level of, 'There are some problems but mummy and daddy are trying to sort them out'. However, we are aware that parents at this time are probably going through a very distressing and upsetting phase of their own and may not be at their best, so such discussions and reassurances may not take place.

Early adolescence (11–16 years)

Children at this age have a more sophisticated grasp of the issues involved but are, perhaps, more aware of the implications in financial and social terms as well as emotional. They may form their own very strong opinions about which parent they perceive to be 'at fault' and in what ways, even if you have taken great care not to talk about blame.

Children of this age can be highly uncommunicative, having left the easy chatter of earlier childhood behind and also because they are starting to organise social lives that most definitely exclude parents. They might not talk much, or even at all, to you about what is going on at home, but could well be getting support from their friends.

Adolescents are becoming aware of their own sexuality, and are starting on the early stages of forming more complex relationships. It is therefore likely that they will be aware of, and form opinions on, sexual relationships, or the sexual nature of you and your ex- or current partner's relationship in a way that younger children would not. This awareness can provide a further layer of complication in their coping with the breakdown of their parents' relationship.

What Children Often Say During This Phase

Mummy and daddy are always arguing. Is it my fault?

Children of all ages have a strong tendency to see the world from their own point of view. They are also inclined to take blame for disharmony that they see around them. Whether they openly express this feeling of responsibility or, indeed, never mention this to parents, it is not at all unusual for children to feel responsible for the difficulties that their parents may be having.

Very young children are obviously unlikely to articulate this belief, but even older children may find it difficult to talk about this openly, if at all. However, this is a classic symptom that we need to be aware of and to deal with at the earliest opportunity.

Children need reassurance that, although there may be difficulties between mum and dad at the moment, this is not the child's fault and in no way are the children responsible for problems the family may be having.

Will mummy stop shouting if I am a really good girl?

Again this is a reflection of the child taking responsibility for family difficulties and, in the absence of a reasonable explanation for why mum or dad are so upset or angry, the child can see themselves as the source of the difficulty and seek to modify their own behaviour in an attempt to appease the parent.

Of course the child's behaviour is not the cause of the parent's problem and, therefore, the parent is likely to carry on being upset, angry or whatever, regardless of the child's efforts. This can lead to unhappiness and frustrations within the child.

Mummy doesn't love daddy any more. Does that mean she doesn't love me?

Again, this is the reflection of the tendency to self-centred thinking on the part of the child but, of course, is a perfectly reasonable extension for the child to make.

The child may have been part of a loving family where mum and dad appeared to care for each other and to love their children. If it has come about that one of the parents has ceased to love the other or, indeed, both parents have ceased to love each other, then certainly, from the child's point of view, it is perfectly possible, and indeed probable that they can stop loving the child.

This is a difficulty to be anticipated and requires parents to give lots of reassurance to the child that, although mum and dad have fallen out and may not be friends any more, they both remain loving, capable parents of the child.

I have seen my dad hit my mum and I hate it.

Obviously not all separations are dealt with in a reasonable or sensible manner. Indeed, family breakdown can occur precisely because of unreasonable behaviour on the part of one partner towards the other.

I suppose it is stating the obvious to say that children can be deeply upset, distressed and disturbed by witnessing domestic violence (see pages 107–8). The repercussions can be severe and have long-lasting effects. It is therefore incumbent upon the parents to ensure that they conduct themselves in such a manner that the children are spared the excesses of their anger and frustration.

I think mum or dad is going to leave. Does this mean I won't see them any more?

Although parents can fall out, and disagree to the extent where they feel they can no longer live together, obviously they will forever remain the parents of their children. However, it is perfectly understandable that a child should feel that a parent capable of leaving the family home will, in all likelihood, never be part of that child's life again.

Clearly, both parents need to be giving reassurance to the child that, although mum and dad won't be living together and, indeed, one of them won't be living as part of the family any more, they will nevertheless always be the parent of the child and will have an ongoing relationship with that child.

In some instances, the absent parent may be able to visit the family home to maintain the relationship. In many other cases, of course, the absent parent is no longer welcome there and, therefore, arrangements will be made for continuing contact between the child and the absent parent elsewhere.

Of course, absent parents certainly have a duty to reassure the child not only in terms of easily spoken words but also by presenting themselves at the prearranged times and places to meet with the child and, indeed, making every effort to ensure that they not only turn up but the time that they spend with the child is meaningful and continues to meet the child's needs.

I hate it when I hear them rowing.

On occasions a child will be present when parents are having arguments or heated discussions about the difficulties in their relationship.

Parents are often well aware that they should seek to have such discussions when the child is not present. However, this can be very difficult with a child in the house and some of the most distressed children I see as a psychologist are those who have overheard parents quarrelling when they were assumed to be tucked up in bed and out of earshot. Such children can become very anxious and fearful when they hear raised voices or other unwelcome noises.

We simply flag up the issue that children who are anywhere in the family home are likely to be able to hear this level of disharmony and parents need to adjust their behaviour accordingly. Arguments may be inevitable but parents need to exercise self control and delay these discussions when matters become heated until the children are elsewhere.

Mummy and daddy don't take me places any more/Mummy and daddy don't talk to me.

These two statements often arise, of course, from the fact that when parents are going through such a difficulty phase in their relationship that their marriage is coming to an end, it can well be the case that their time, effort and energy is taken up simply surviving from day to day and trying to deal with the repercussions and implications of the relationship breakdown. Very often, through no fault of their own other than simply not thinking about it, parents can retreat within themselves and simply withdraw from the family, including the parent who will be staying with the children. Even within normal levels of low mood that do not amount to clinical depression parents can find that they do withdraw from their children.

The very simplistic solution to this is, of course, that parents need to ensure that they maintain the continuity of their relationships with their children and that they remain part of the daily dialogue of family life. In particular the parent who is likely to be absent in the future needs to be maintaining that dialogue now and actively seeking out the child or children to reassure them that relationships will be preserved.

You could cut the atmosphere with a knife.

This sort of statement is usually made by an older child but even younger children are very adept at picking up on atmospheres within the family home.

Although parents may be doing their level best to deal with their relationship difficulties in as reasonable a manner as possible and, indeed, may be limiting their discussions, whether heated or calm, to those times when the children are not present, it is often a source of great surprise when they realise how aware the children are, however young, of the difficulties that their mum and dad are experiencing.

Even very young children are perfectly capable of sensing these atmospheres and, consequently, become somewhat unsettled and distressed.

Mum/dad tells me all about their problems. I hate it.

We have so far sought to emphasise that it is important for parents to maintain a dialogue with their children and offer as much information as they can cope with at their respective ages, coupled with masses of reassurance that, though there may be significant changes in their lives, they will remain loved by both mum and dad. However, in extreme cases one or other of the parents can actually seek to over-engage with the children and, in effect, try to get them on their side. Though this is understandable, most children love both parents and are not equipped to deal with this situation.

Over-engaging can not only sow the seeds for considerable damage in the relationship between the child and the other parent, but there is also the likelihood of a significant backlash for the parent using the child as a confidante, in that the child may avoid that parent out of a wish to avoid the intimacy. It could escalate to the point that the child places the other parent in a much more reasonable light and arranges to distance themselves from the confiding parent.

What is going to happen to me?

Clearly this is the crucial question for most children in the situation of family breakdown.

Children are aware that life is changing, that things are probably never going to be quite the same again, and are clearly very worried about what effect this is going to have on them directly. Their understanding of the possible impact is, of course, influenced by the child's age and stage of development; an older child will obviously have a more subtle grasp than a younger child of the likely social, economic, emotional and educational implications of the family breakdown.

However, the actual detail of the breakdown will depend, to a large extent, on whether the child will be able to remain in the family home, or whether the house will have to be sold and the family move on, probably to less favourable financial and social circumstances. Clearly moves of this type might involve questions about moving schools, losing old friends and having to make new friends. All in all, this can be a very worrying and frightening time for children.

The parents may have entered into the divorce process without fully thinking through the implications and it could simply be the case that neither of them is fully aware of what the future will hold. In that situation, other than reassuring the child that they will be loved and cared for, both by the parent who will continue to live with them and the absent parent, it may simply not be possible at this time to give reassurances about future living and financial arrangements or even education arrangements.

Clearly these are matters that should be thought through at the earliest possible stage but, given the nature of life and its difficulties, they often are not.

I don't want things to change.

Experience suggests that children prefer to maintain the status quo. Put another way, having even dysfunctional parents or parents who find it difficult to get on can appear better to the children than one parent leaving, and they will often do whatever they can if they think it will ensure mum and dad will stay together. Even children whose parents have been apart for quite some time, and who appear to be fully reconciled to the fact that mum and dad are not living together, often say that they would still like mum or dad to return to the family and things to be as they were previously, even though they understand that it would be very difficult.

Sometimes, though, children can understand that it would be better for mum and dad not to be living together, as long as they can maintain a relationship between both parents.

Tasks for Parents Contemplating Separation

1. From the outset make the children your number one priority

It is often the case that in relationship breakdowns, one parent comes to the notion of divorce before the other does. It might be that the initiating parent can no longer contemplate living with their partner, or has met someone else with whom they would rather be living. Even at this stage, though, thought needs to be given as to what the implications of this are for the children.

Earlier we referred to the social, emotional and financial practicalities that need to be thought through to ensure the children's future well-being. When both parents realise that the relationship is beyond salvaging and divorce is likely, then it is incumbent upon them both to put the needs of the children to the fore during any planning for the future.

Unfortunately, at this time one or both parents are likely to be going through a period of such turmoil and emotional distress that they are simply overwhelmed and unable to think through these complex issues. Nevertheless, it is essential that these issues are part of the early agenda.

The message conveyed here is that parents have to step back from being devastated by their own emotional fears and practical worries and that they need to be constantly reflecting upon how their behaviour as individuals, or as parents, is impacting on the children both at the time and in the medium and long term. Of course it is much easier to write this than it is to carry it out.

2. Plan for the future

At the time of a relationship breakdown, planning for the future is of course incredibly difficult. If the parents are able to continue to work together from the outset to ensure the well-being of their children then there is an increased likelihood that future planning can be undertaken to minimise the impact of the breakdown on the children.

Without repeating everything I have said above, it is clear that children can find this a very distressing time and they need massive amounts of reassurance that, although there will be significant changes in their life in that one parent will be moving out to live elsewhere, nevertheless the love and care that they have received from both parents will be ongoing. Unfortunately, it is very common indeed for the parents not to be able to work together, in which case each parent individually needs to be giving these reassurances to the child.

It is very easy indeed at this stage for parents to play one off against the other and to say disparaging and very hurtful comments about the other partner. While many of these comments may be deserved, nevertheless the child does not need to be embroiled in those sorts of issues and needs to be protected as far as possible. I am not suggesting that the child or children should be told nothing. They should be told that mum and dad are not getting along and that mum or dad will be moving out. They should also be helped to understand that, although that parent is not now a very good partner to the mum or dad, nevertheless, they can still remain a perfectly good parent to the child.

If the parents are able to work together, of course, practical matters can be resolved to minimise the impact upon the children and, as far as possible, to ensure continuity in their lives. For example, financial and educational arrangements should be made as quickly as possible. The major difficulty for children occurs where parents are not able to work together to ensure their well-being, and where the disharmony between the parents is such that no communication takes place and matters are simply left to drift with issues not being resolved quickly. When this is the case, the child is left in turmoil, where their little life is not only being unsettled by the absence of perhaps a loved parent, but also the implication is that everything else is in turmoil too, with the child not knowing where they are going to be living, who they are going to be with, and how matters are to proceed.

3. Both parents work together on reassuring the child

The task of the parent is to be fully aware of the emotional, social, economic and other implications on the children and to seek to disengage from the marital relationship in as reasonable a manner as possible, maintaining behaviour within reasonable limits.

Both parents need to be giving positive assurance to the child or children that, although mum and dad have fallen out and don't want to be living together any more, they nevertheless both love the child and will continue to do whatever they can to ensure the child is okay. If the parents are not able to do this together, then both parents, individually, need to give this reassurance and conduct themselves in a manner such that the children's emotional needs continue to be met. The clear message from both parents must be 'We still love you, even if we don't love each other any more'.

It is also helpful for a child to understand, as far as possible within the limits of his or her own development, that although mum and dad may be angry, upset and worried at times, it is not directed at the child or because of anything he or she has done. It is also acceptable to acknowledge that, at times, that anger may spill over on to the child, but reassurances must be given that it is simply because mummy or daddy is so upset.

Summary

We can see that planning for separation and divorce that involves children is a very complicated affair indeed. Parents have a set of tasks to carry out which, under normal circumstances, would usually be well within their capacities. Unfortunately, of course, all of this is being asked of the parents at a time when they may be very distressed and angry indeed. Nevertheless, as parents they have as far as possible to control themselves, their own emotions and their behaviour, to ensure that they continue to act as responsible parents for their children.

From the very earliest stages the parent or parents need to be placing the welfare of the children to the fore, ensuring that the child's emotional, social, economic and educational needs remain the number one priority. Neglecting these issues can have a serious and profound effect on a child and can, indeed, lead to long-term difficulties for the youngster if not dealt with in a very sensitive and sensible manner during these early stages.

Examples are given above of the sorts of issues that children of families where divorce is imminent have raised. These issues are very serious indeed for the child experiencing them and need to be taken on board. The implications of not recognising these potential difficulties and not dealing with them in a sensitive and sensible manner invariably mean that the children suffer much more than they need to.

I am very much aware of the parents' own humanity and frailty and I do not wish to punish parents simply because their marriage or relationship has come to an end. But, although they may be frightened and upset at this phase, they are at least old enough to understand what is happening. The child can also feel all of those fears and the distress and upset, but has no power or control over their destiny. What I am suggesting is that thoughtful, careful planning and being aware of one's own and the other parent's behaviour can of itself lead to children experiencing much less distress during what is clearly a very difficult phase of change in their little lives.

This leads us on to the next phase in this process, which is the separation itself.

CHAPTER 3

The Split

In the broadest sense, when one of the parents leaves the family home it is simply one step in the process of separation and divorce. Nevertheless, it can be viewed as a special case in that it forms a specific event in the life of the family, and, indeed, the life of the child.

The significance of preparatory work

The specific impact of the split in any particular family depends to a large extent on the success, or otherwise, of the preparatory work undertaken as discussed in Chapter 2. In reality, of course, we have to look at several possible scenarios.

In some families there will have been a great deal of preparatory work between the parents and between the parents and their children. Ideally this work will have been good and positive and will have reassured the children that, although mum and dad no longer wish to live together, the children remain loved by both parents and both parents will do whatever is necessary to ensure their children's emotional and other well-being into the future.

In other families preparatory work will have been undertaken, but less successfully in that the disruption and dysfunction between the parents has spilled over on to the children and the children have not been able to receive reassuring messages from both parents. It may be the case that one parent is trying to battle on regardless and care for the children while the other parent is simply unable to.

For yet other families it may be the case that the opportunity for preparation has just not been available in that one partner has, completely unexpectedly, revealed to the other that they want out of the relationship now, perhaps because he or she has become involved with someone else. Clearly this sudden crisis revelation is likely to be a great shock and upset to the parent receiving the news, and of course to the children who are having to cope with mum and dad's relationship falling apart at the same time as wondering what on earth is going to happen to themselves.

I suppose for completeness we should also acknowledge the other possibility which, thankfully, is not that common, whereby one partner simply leaves the family home as usual but does not return, just saying: 'I've had enough. I'm going.'

When considering each of the above scenarios, we need to take into account that we are not dealing with children as a homogenous group, but with children at different ages and stages who each come with their own personality and life experiences that have shaped them in their ability to cope with whatever difficulties they are faced with. As well as this, if there is more than one child in the family, it might be expected that each will have a different relationship with either mum or dad. Age, quality of relationship and resilience can all have significant impact on how individuals or families will respond to the challenge of the actual split.

No matter how we have arrived at this point, the day comes when it becomes real that a parent or partner has gone. Sometimes it is the case that a parent leaves and there is a subsequent reconciliation, but for the purpose of this discussion we are looking upon the split as being the end of the marriage. The time has come to face up to the reality of the situation and reconcile oneself with the fact that the marriage has ended and that a partner or parent has left.

Putting promises into action

Now is the time for the promises made jointly by the parents during the breakdown phase to be put into practice. The parents will have already identified, between themselves and with the children in age-appropriate ways, which areas of life are likely to continue as before, and which areas of life are likely to change.

Simply looking at the emotional, social, educational and financial scenarios we can see that mum and dad need to continue to give reassurance in words, but now, and perhaps more importantly, also by their actions. Emotionally, of course, the children need to know that they continue to be loved by both their parents and that it is perfectly acceptable to either parent that their children express their love for the other parent.

Children of school age will have been fully informed of the issues regarding their school attendance and plans will have been made for them to stay within their existing school or to transfer to another if there is a need to move family home. If you have not already done so, the school should be informed of the new circumstances under which the family is functioning, so that school too can provide any support that the child needs. Of course, both the parent who will continue to care on a day-to-day basis for the child, plus the absent parent, will still maintain their relationship with the school, and one would have every expectation that they will continue to liase with the school in terms of ensuring their children's best interests are maintained.

While finances will not necessarily be discussed directly with the children, these issues will have a direct impact on the children and the lifestyle to which they have become accustomed. While family splits often lead to less money being available to the children, nevertheless the impact on the children needs to have been thought through so that at least the children's core activities can be maintained; children can be expensive little beings and their ongoing activities need to be financed as well as keeping a roof over their head.

Social aspects are again a reflection of living arrangements, to a large extent. If the children are to remain where they were living before the split, then it is hoped that ongoing friendships and contact with neighbours will be maintained. It is also to be expected that wider family members, such as grandparents, aunts, uncles and cousins, would still be available to the children irrespective of which 'family' (mum's or dad's) they belong to. Particularly with this category, there can be a strong temptation to take sides, but individuals should be asked to recognise that this is not particularly helpful and they should simply provide the support that the children need.

Contact with the absent parent

From the moment of split, the very important beginnings of contact arrangements begin to come into practice. I suppose the rule of thumb here is that, as far as is humanly possible, it is incumbent upon both parents to keep to the good home, school and social routines that the children are used to. Both parents, and particularly the now absent parent, must ensure that if they have said they are coming to see a child, or they are having a child come to see them, then that arrangement is kept to. There are few things more distressing for a child than to be let down by an absent parent who simply fails to show or who habitually turns up late. If arrangements simply cannot be kept then this needs to be discussed fully and frankly with the child, and the parent caring for the child, to ensure that no message is given to the child, however inadvertently, that in some way they are not loved and cared for or are second best.

The emotional impact of the split

It is highly likely that if parents have gone through a good preparation phase they will be able to move through this pivotal point of the split on to the phase that will be discussed in Chapter Four. But however well the split has been anticipated, and however well the parents feel they have prepared themselves for the final move from the family home, it is inevitable that the actual event will represent, at least, a significant blip for the parents that may resurrect emotions they thought they had under control. It is not at all unusual for feelings of anger, fear and hurt to re-emerge at this point. This is a natural human reaction to the stress and change of circumstance, but nevertheless, forewarned and thus forearmed, parents can anticipate that this is likely to occur and seek to minimise its impact on the children.

However, for the children too, no matter how well they have been prepared for mum or dad leaving, when it finally happens it is a very important point in their young lives. The added stress and unsettling nature of mum or dad leaving needs to be recognised and, of course, not only positive reassurance given but also any deterioration in conduct recognised for what it is and managed with understanding and firmness, rather than thinking of it simply as poor behaviour.

If preparation for splitting has not gone well, and parents have been so caught up in their own emotional world that they have not been able to look to the emotional as well as other needs of the children, then it is highly likely that this dysfunction will continue during and after the split. In this scenario, the children may have watched their parents becoming less and less happy with one another and becoming more estranged, and in the process the children are likely to be suffering as outlined in Chapter 2. They may have little sense of any areas of continuity in their lives. They may simply not know what the future is likely to bring.

Paradoxically, however, this split can be a positive experience even in those families where the preparation has not gone well. For example, it could well be the case that a partner moving from the family home actually brings about a significant change, or indeed an improvement, for the parent who is staying at home with the children. Finally being without the day-to-day trauma of living with a partner who is preparing to leave may free up the remaining parent and allow them to accept the reality of the loss of the relationship, to feel the distress in whatever way it is they wish to feel it, but then move on to disengaging from that relationship as rapidly as possible. In the process that parent may feel a great sense of relief and, as such, be able once again to refocus on the care that their children need. In these circumstances children can flourish very well indeed.

The danger to be aware of at this point is that inadvertently, or indeed sometimes on purpose, the parent can begin to poison the mind of the child against the absent parent. We make the point several times in this book that being a bad partner does not necessarily mean that you are a bad parent. Most parents can accept this and, although they may feel furious to the extreme at being abandoned by their partner, they can, nevertheless, recognise that that absent partner is still a good parent to their children. While it is perfectly appropriate for the children to be aware of their mum's or dad's unhappiness at the other partner, nevertheless children need to be actively encouraged to maintain their relationship with the absent parent. On the other hand, of course, it is the responsibility of the absent parent to ensure that they remain as positive as possible about the parent who is providing day-to-day care for the children. If this is not done, it can easily be seen that there is the potential for a big split in the family from which it may never recover.

One often hears about parental rights, and the fact that parents feel that they have the right to do this, that or the other with regard to the welfare of the children. To my mind, the main issue is really one of parental responsibility. This is one time when the parents do have ultimate responsibility for the welfare of the children to ensure that they support them whatever their feelings regarding their former partner.

At the point of split, even in those families where there has been good preparation, the husband or wife moving out of the family home can add to the existing dysfunction. People can find themselves very surprised by how upset they are, even though they had thought they wanted the husband or wife to leave as soon as possible. The act of leaving, or being left, can feel so final that people are bereft. This feeling is frequently short lived, but it needs to be recognised as a possibility.

When the split comes as a major surprise to one partner, in the sense that the other announced suddenly that he or she wanted to end the relationship for some reason, this can be a particularly fraught form of separation. It is highly likely that the parent who has been faced with this revelation will simply be reeling from the shock of it all. Clearly there will be little time to prepare the children for the parent leaving and it may well be the case that the preparation described in Chapter 2 needs to be condensed into a very short period indeed, or even dealt with following the departure of one of the parents. How well people recover from this news is clearly dependent upon the pre-existing relationship, their individual temperament and previous life experience. Some parents are extremely resilient and, while shocked, stunned and quite disbelieving about what has happened to themselves and their world, are nevertheless still able to put the needs of their children to the fore. Others may simply be unable to properly consider the emotional well-being of the children and in this situation it is likely that the family will need significant support from others, including wider family and/or friends.

What Children Often Say During This Phase

Where has daddy gone? Where is he living?

Clearly one of the worries for children is what has become of the parent who has left home. Part of the planning phase would be helping a child to understand that daddy or mummy was moving out but that they will be living in reasonable circumstances. Tied in with this, of course, is the child's need to know that dad or mum will be returning at some stage to see them, or they will be going off to see mum or dad, even though they will no longer be living together.

Will he be okay?

Again, this follows on from the above, where the child needs to be reassured that dad or mum will be fine even though they are no longer living in the family home. It is recognised that this can be very difficult for the remaining parent, who may still be harbouring feelings of anger and resentment, but nevertheless, as far as is humanly possible the parent needs to support the child in maintaining that relationship with the absent parent.

Who is he living with?

How to answer this can be complex. For example, it may be the case that dad has moved to live on his own. He may be staying with another family, perhaps his own parents. He may now be living with a new partner. Especially if the separation has been acrimonious and communication has been bad, the remaining parent may only have an address for her former partner, and for a time at least may simply not know any other details of his living arrangements.

Which of these scenarios applies will have different implications for the child, not just in their knowledge of such things, but how it will impact upon them and their future relationship with the absent parent. If dad is living on his own, then it should be fairly easy to arrange contact arrangements for him to visit the child. If he is no longer welcome in the child's home, the child can visit dad in his new accommodation, provided it is suitable. If dad has moved in with another family, it is very important that its members do not take sides in this process but simply support the child in retaining a relationship with both mum and dad. It is certainly not appropriate for family members to pass comment on the parent who cares for the child on a day-to-day basis. The third scenario raises its own difficulties in that, if dad has left to go and live with someone else, the child or children are not only coping with dad moving out but also are faced with dad apparently replacing mum with someone else. In addition, they can be faced with their parents' sexuality at a time when they find this very difficult to cope with.

Why is mummy still crying all the time?

Even following a good preparation phase, where the split was anticipated and where planning had been carefully carried out, the final act of leaving home can have a very negative affect on the remaining parent. They can be surprised at how bereft they feel, even if intellectually they know that the relationship finally concluding is for the best.

Children can find this phase very difficult in that, perhaps months earlier, during the initial upset, they may have seen mum or dad very upset but watched them all the time, planning, talking and working together for the separation. When the time comes when one parent leaves, the child may assume that the remaining parent, who will be caring for the child on a day-to-day basis, is already reconciled and happy with that situation. To find oneself faced instead with a mum or dad whose mood has dropped and who is simply not coping as well as they had been previously, can doubly compound the problem for the child. Having said that, of course, we are only human, and providing this phase of upset and distress does not last for too long, the children will survive perfectly well.

Again dialogue with the child is important and, in an age-appropriate way, they need to be reassured that the upset is because of the parent moving out and not because of anything the child has done. Remind the child that in a while you will be okay again, and meanwhile could they bear with you while you cope as best you can.

Of course the children too will be needing care and support at this time and their own feelings, which we anticipated in Chapter 2, need to be recognised and dealt with in as supportive a manner as is possible.

I hate daddy for going!

I think no matter what the circumstances of the split, it is perfectly understandable that a child should feel very angry towards the parent who has left. The child may blame this parent for the breakdown and the general disruption of the family.

As far as possible, the child needs to be reassured that daddy has left because mum and dad don't love each other any more and that this has little, if anything, to do with the children. Despite mum's and dad's problems, the child or children are still loved by dad.

Nevertheless, the parent moving out needs to anticipate this sort of reaction. With reassurance from both parents and by witnessing the parents' actions over time following the split, they will come to see that dad is not a monster but he actually means it when he says he loves them, and he means it when he says he will keep the relationship going and that he will see them regularly. In time they will accept that perhaps dad is a person for whom they can have these negative emotions but will move on to re-establishing the pre-existing, more positive relationship.

I hate you for driving him away!

The other side of the issue considered above is that it is perhaps the parent who remains who receives the backlash from the child or children. In some children's eyes, particularly if they have had a very strong relationship with the parent who has left, the remaining parent can be seen as the villain of the piece and the person who actively drove mum or dad away. Of course this can be particularly hurtful if the parent still there and caring for the children feels that they are the 'wronged' partner.

Nevertheless, the same sort of action as in the case above should be applied, whereby constant reassurance from both parents, and the children seeing over time that mum and dad still care for and love them and can still maintain a relationship with them, will enable the children to work through their anger in a way that leads to the re-establishment of pre-existing better relationships.

In both of these scenarios, it is the parents' job to recognise that these feelings are legitimate and that the children are saying what they are saying out of the hurt and distress they are experiencing. One must guard against letting the children think they are wrong to feel this way. This can be very difficult, of course, for parents who are undergoing their own traumas but it is, nevertheless, really the only reasonable way forward.

Does daddy still love me?

Again this is a worry we have addressed throughout. If it is the case that a dad or mum can leave the family, and that the parents no longer love each other, then it is a perfectly reasonable extension for the child to think that mum or dad will stop loving them too.

However, over time, with words but more importantly by actions, children can see that they will be loved by both parents. It is important for all concerned to give lots of reassurance to the child.

Will I ever see my daddy again?

Again, in the early stages one can see that this is the reflection of the child's insecurity and the fact that, at that point, he or she has not been able to see the adults translate what has been said into action.

For all of us, of course, words can be cheap and it is actions that lead us to believe that what people have said is genuine. From that point of view, it is only over time, and with repeated good experiences, that the children will come to accept and see that daddy still loves them and that he will remain part of their lives.

What will I tell my friends?

While difficulties within the family are hard for children to cope with, sharing those difficulties with people outside of their family can be even harder, even though it is a sad fact that so many children are involved in relationship breakdowns. Certainly in any particular school there will already be several children who are known to be living in a family where mum and dad are no longer together. Familiarity with breakdown, and an awareness that other children have ongoing relationships with absent parents, can make the transition into a single-parent family far easier than it was when divorce was more unusual.

Experience suggests that with sensitive handling on the part of parents, as well as good ongoing support from schools and others involved with the family, a child can be helped to understand that mum and dad not living together does not make a child particularly odd or particularly different from their friends. The child should be reassured that they remain loved by their parents, that they will have ongoing contact with other family members, and that their teachers will have been told of the family difficulties so that they can support the child at school.

Nevertheless, the act of informing friends themselves need to be very carefully carried out. Parents of young children need only tell the friends parents and ask them to do what is necessary for their own child and yours to ensure continuity of the friendship. The friends of middle-childhood age and beyond children can simply be told, by you, their parents, or by your children themselves if they wish, that mum and dad have fallen out, dad or mum is living somewhere else, and perhaps whatever they are feeling about this. Older children are very likely to want to tell their friends themselves in their own words. This is an area where you need to be particularly sensitive to what is appropriate for your children, taking into account their age, maturity and personality. It may be necessary to ask your child for permission before the changed family circumstances are made known to their friends.

Although it is well known that children can be incredibly cruel to one another, it is also surprising how supportive they can be when the child is going through a difficult phase such as this. Above all, your child should be told that he or she will not be judged by anyone because of the changed family circumstances.

Why has he gone to live with her children and left me?

One of the most difficult scenarios to deal with is when mum or dad has left home and set up home fairly quickly with another partner who has children.

Again, perfectly understandably, children can be very confused as to why dad should no longer be able to live with them, and yet has gone off to live with, to all intents and purposes, another family, so must be taking care of those children while no longer being in a position to care for his own.

This issue will be discussed at greater length in Chapter 6 when we look at new individuals entering the children's lives but, even at this early stage, some children can be faced with this situation. It requires a great deal of sensitive handling from the remaining parent, who may of course be experiencing very much the same confusion, anger and hurt as the children themselves in this regard. At the same time, for the children's well-being, they need to maintain as positive a role as they can regarding dad. It is under these circumstances, in particular, that ongoing reassurance, active commitment to contact and, above all, ensuring that the child has time alone with the absent parent as well as with the new partner and children, are vital.

I never liked him anyway. He was just a guy I lived with.

The above statement is often a reflection of the fact that not all relationships between children and parents are positive.

It may well be the case that the children have lived in an unhappy environment for really quite some time, where the family was dysfunctional at some level in advance of recognising that they were in the throes of divorce. Children are extremely adept at sensing when thing are not going well within a family, even though they may not have an in-depth understanding of why; certainly their understanding of function and dysfunction pre-dates their ability to verbalise it. So it is not unusual to find that children have made up their own minds about their parents but it is revealed only at a time of crisis.

Parents can find themselves very surprised indeed by their own children's reactions, and the revelations and insights they have into how well or otherwise the parents have been functioning as parents. It is not unusual to hear a child say quite negative things about a parent that are very much in line with the views of the other parent, even though it has never been verbalised between the parent and child before.

Under such circumstances, of course, it may be very difficult indeed to maintain a relationship between the child and the absent parent. Realistically, there may be nothing at all that can be done; the child's feelings for the parent, even before the break-up, are so negative that there is no previous good relationship to try to resurrect.

It could be that the remaining parent, especially if they were very hurt by the split and feel they have been wronged, feels quite pleased at apparently being preferred by the child. However, it would be counterproductive to use what your child has said as a go-ahead to form an alliance with him or her against your former partner.

This kind of statement could also indicate that the child is protecting him or herself from pain (see pages 56–7).

I don't blame him for going; I wish I could.

I suppose this is the reverse scenario to the one above, where the child is now living with the parent whom they feel is the less preferred one, while the more loved parent leaves. In that situation, the parent who stays behind can get the backlash of the child's anger and upset that may be historic, in the sense that they may never have had a particularly good relationship with the child. It may also be the case that the remaining parent gets the anger from the child that could be directed at either parent or both, but is focused on that parent simply because they are there. A child in extreme distress may, in effect, even be saying 'I want to run away from it all' or 'I don't want to live'.

Whatever the truth of the matter, both parents, but particularly the absent parent, are going to need to provide a great deal of support to reassure the child that he or she remains loved and cared for by both parents. Of course, this will probably be happening at a time when both parents are far from happy with one another. Nevertheless, putting the child's needs to the fore, they need to ensure that the child's angry outbursts are understood for what they are, which will have some basis in history but also need to be appreciated as an expression of their current emotional state.

As with the previous scenario, it is essential that the absent parent guards against the temptation to make more of apparent favouritism than they should. The child may not yet have settled into the new home arrangements and may be feeling that an alternative could only be an improvement, in the same way that many children say they would have liked their parents to have stayed together even though they knew theirs was not a happy family. It should not be seen as any kind of point-scoring or as further justification for the split. Indeed, a parent who is no longer in the family home should appreciate that the remaining parent is having to deal with this additional stress on a day-to-day basis, and may be feeling very hurt if the child has actually expressed this feeling in so many words.

Tasks for Parents at the Time of a Parent Leaving Home

1. Both parents remain responsible for their children's welfare

If the family has been able to go through a good preparation before the separation, then the parents must now turn promises into reality in all areas – emotional, social, educational and financial. While it is recognised that this a particularly stressful time for the parents, nevertheless they have to remain united and work together to ensure that their children are okay. It is recognised that, while talking with the children is desirable, in reality it is by their behaviour that the children will come to believe and to trust their parents beyond the separation. All the words in the world will mean nothing if the children are let down by their parents.

If the parents have not been able to go through a good preparation before the separation, then they have to, as quickly as possible, seek to salvage the situation. They need to recognise that their own relationship is over, but that their responsibilities to the children remain and, therefore, individually if not collectively, they have to refocus on the needs of the children. In a sense both parents are also struggling to cope with the loss of the relationship, and it is recognised that the pain is multiplied when parents have to help their children through the process at the same time.

2. Take action to preserve relationships

This is a time of great sensitivity and there is a danger that the children can be influenced by one parent into taking sides and in the process demonise the other. Obviously the children's relationship with their parents is based in history, although that is no doubt being affected by the current trauma. It is the job of both parents to ensure that, if at all possible, the children's relationship with each parent is operating at its best. This, of course, is on the assumption that this is what is best for the children, even if not necessarily for the parents.

When revelations of one parent wanting to leave the relationship come unexpectedly, leaving little or no time for any preparation and with lots of things happening at once, this is clearly a time of crisis for the entire family when the parents will not be functioning at their best to deal with the children. Therefore, much of the work we talked about earlier to prepare for separation may have to be done post-separation; the fact that the parents have already separated does not mean that this work does not need to be done, but sadly that the work is probably going to have to be done separately rather than together. If at all possible, the parents need to resurrect some degree of working relationship in the best interests of the children.

3. Understand your children's behaviour

Children may express their anger and upset in many and varied ways, some of which have been identified above. The task for the parents is to recognise what the child is doing, and remember that they know their child better than anyone else does. They know their personal and family histories and how relationships have functioned in the past. Consequently, if a child says 'I hate daddy, it's his fault' or 'I hate you, it's your fault', how this is interpreted and responded to depends on this history. For example, if a child has had a perfectly good relationship with a father to whom they now express a great deal of anger, the task is to help the children express and recognise that anger, but then seek to move on and resurrect the pre-existing good relationship. If the relationship between the parent and child was poor, and the child continues to express anger and hostility towards that parent, then perhaps it is a expression of reality, making it very difficult to form any positive relationship with that parent.

4. Be sensitive to your children's need

Recognise that children are individuals and are different in terms of their personality and of their relationship with each parent. Different children in one family may have positive or negative relationships with a particular parent. Whatever the qualities of these relationships, each of them is legitimate and needs to be recognised.

Of course, this can create conflict between siblings, in that if one remains loyal or loving towards one particular parent, and the other takes against that parent, then we have a further source of conflict. However, even in this situation it is the parent's task to step in to resolve difficulties, rather than leaving the children to their own devices.

5. Continue to put your children first

Parents have rights, but more importantly they have responsibilities. Those responsibilities last throughout childhood and need to be taken seriously, whether or not that parent continues to live with the other parent of the child. A recurring theme is that, while it is recognised that parents have their own emotional needs and they may be very upset indeed by the breakdown in the relationship, the task of the parent is to take a step back and think carefully about what is best for the children of the family, even if this means doing or saying things that they do not particularly feel. One could imagine a mum or dad, very upset and angry with a partner but nevertheless seeking to maintain as positive a relationship as possible between that child and that parent, simply on the basis that they believe that is what is in the best interest of the child, striving to appear upbeat and positive about that parent even if at that point in time this doesn't reflect their own thoughts and feelings.

6. Acknowledge the significance of the actual split

In contrast to other aspects of the process of separation and divorce, the act of leaving home can be viewed as much more of an event than a process. Even parents who have worked towards the moving out in as positive a manner as possible can be very surprised at how upsetting and distressing this moving out can be for the whole family.

7. Remember that you are only human

Accept that none of us is perfect, even at the best of times. Separating parents will make mistakes along the way. Provided that they remedy those mistakes as quickly as possible, with loving ongoing care the children will survive perfectly well.

Summary

Parents are only human and they have their own thoughts and feelings to contend with. However, the overriding message is that, while divorce and the moving away of one partner have become a perfectly acceptable way of life to which very little, if any, blame is attached, nevertheless being a parent is being a parent forever.

Because of this, at times parents have to put to one side their own, perhaps very negative, feelings towards the other parent and help the children work through their own feelings so that they can maintain as reasonable and as positive a relationship as possible with the absent parent and, indeed, the parent who continues to provide day-to-day care. Anything less than this is to the children's disadvantage.

CHAPTER 4

Moving On

The assumption by now is that the marriage or relationship has achieved a stage where it has irrevocably broken down, and the couple have now split, one parent having left the family home. The individuals within the family now have to deal with the repercussions of the family breakdown and split, and seek to move forward in their lives, adjusting to the new circumstances under which they will be living.

As has been emphasised throughout this book, this phase is simply part of an ongoing process and the time it takes to reach will vary. For some the split will have occurred after perhaps many months from when it was first recognised that relationships in the family were not going well and the parents tried to deal with that in whatever way they felt appropriate. The children had been helped, or hindered, during that phase to adjust to the fact that their parents were separating. For others the breakdown of the family, and the split, will have occurred in a very short period of time. No matter how long or short a time the family has had to adjust to the split, it has happened, and now the family members have to move on. In this chapter, I want to look at families grieving the loss of the marriage and the leaving of one parent.

It should be recognised that, when considering these issues, each individual will move through the adjustment processes involved in their own way and at their own speed, and it is highly likely that individuals will find themselves at odds with others in the family, simply because they are at different stages in the adjustment process.

Grieving the loss

It would be useful to repeat here the simple, but nevertheless useful, model of grieving.

- Stage 1: accept the reality of the loss.

- Stage 2: feel the pain of the loss.

- Stage 3: disinvest in that relationship.

- Stage 4: reinvest in other relationships.

In terms of the understanding of the 'moving on' process, we can consider these phases of grieving and its impact on family members.

Accepting the reality that the relationship is over

It is worth asking at this point what the 'reality' is. Of course, for the parents concerned, the reality for one parent is often that they have left a relationship that they no longer wish to be in and, indeed, that parent may have already embarked on another relationship. The other parent may also have achieved this thinking but, on the other hand, it is more likely that they are still trying to come to terms with the fact that their most significant relationship is really over. Of course, this partner cannot move on through the grieving process to disengage from that relationship and develop other relationships. They may find themselves 'stuck' for many days, weeks, months or in some cases even years, failing to accept that the relationship has gone forever and may continue to wish, or expect, that their partner will return.

For the child, or children of the family, the task is somewhat different. As has been emphasised throughout this book, although the parents can separate and move on from each other's lives, once a parent always a parent, and the children, therefore, will seek to accept a different reality to that of their individual parents. Mum or dad may be living elsewhere, but, nevertheless, the child has not lost that parent as a parent and the relationship the child has with that parent will be ongoing. Therefore, the children are accepting a quite different reality from that of their parents. This mismatch in reality can cause difficulties within the family.

If there is more than one child, the children cannot necessarily be considered as a homogenous group. Each of them will be coming to terms with their new reality and it may, of course, come at different times for different children, even of the same age.

Feeling the pain of the relationship breakdown

However, and whenever, an individual arrives at the reality that a parent or partner has moved out and will no longer be a physical presence in the family on a day-to-day basis, that individual then has to deal with the emotional consequence.

In this second phase – allowing oneself to feel the pain of the reality of the separation – we must again recognise that different people will feel different things at different times. For some individuals involved in the separation, the separation itself, and the reality that the separation is irreversible, may be looked upon as something of a relief. This may be particularly the case for the parent who wanted out of the relationship, but the parent who wanted the relationship to continue may also be relieved since they are now removed from the daily trauma of seeking to retrieve a relationship that is, in reality, lost. For the children, too, it may come as a change for the better as they are no longer facing, on a daily or regular basis, their parents squabbling and being upset with one another.

However, accepting the reality of the new situation can also result in overwhelming feelings of anger, hurt and distress, resulting in low moods. The partner who has left may still experience negative feelings – perhaps guilt, or resentment towards the partner who was unable to fulfil their needs. A partner who feels wronged or who wished the relationship to continue may have invested a great deal of energy in trying to sustain the relationship and is now crushed by the realisation that it was a lost cause.

Understandably, children can become very unsettled in this phase. They will need to be reassured, in both word and deed, that they still have an ongoing relationship with both parents. As indicated in the previous chapter, contact becomes a very important issue, and regular attendance of the parent at the family home or the children visiting the absent parent can be a source of comfort and assurance that the absent parent is okay.

Dealing with the pain of the loss

In reality, it is impossible to protect the children at all times from distress. It is simply acknowledged that the children will feel, at times, upset or angry and may find it very difficult indeed to find a way to air that anger and upset. However, there are two classic phrases that can be applied to understand and deal with these emotions:

Put anger where it belongs

Unexpressed anger leads to depression so it is essential that anger is put where it belongs.

Putting anger in its context

For a parent or child who is feeling very angry, it is important to identify, as quickly as possible, what it is that one is angry about or whom one is angry with.

If it is the absent parent who has caused the problem, then it is legitimate for that anger to be directed towards the absent parent, be it by the other parent or the children. However, it is often the case that we spray our anger around indiscriminately or direct it at the nearest and safest person. Thus children have a tendency to express their anger to the remaining parent who is still affording them day-to-day care. By the same token, the parent charged with the responsibility for the children may find that they are venting their anger towards the children.

While this tendency is recognised, it is of course undesirable and it is important that steps are taken to curtail the situation as soon as you are aware that it is happening. Children must be reassured that, though the parent is upset and angry, it is not at them. In these circumstances the support of family and friends can be invaluable; because they are more remote from the situation it will not impact on them if parents express their anger to them.

As indicated, children, too, will be having their own thoughts and feelings and may be directing anger at the parent. An important, but fairly obvious, comment at this point is that it is much better for the child to ventilate anger, even if it is inappropriately directed, than trying to bottle it up and not finding a way to express it. After any outburst the child should be talked to and helped to understand that the parent has not taken it personally and recognises that the cause is ongoing upset about the absent parent.

The absent parent may not be a target for that anger for several reasons. It may be a reflection on the fact that they are simply not around to experience the child's anger when it happens, but it is just as probable that, when the child is with the absent parent, he or she will suppress anger for fear that expressing it would put future contact at risk.

Recognising and dispelling anger

When the parent, or parents, or children have come to some understanding of the reality of the situation and are experiencing the negative emotions that go with it, if they are not recognised and dealt with or ventilated in some way, then it is highly likely that the individual will seek to bury those emotions deep down inside. Under those circumstances the mood will lower and the parent or child will simply not understand why they are feeling so awful and upset.

The pain and trauma we feel when we lose a relationship, or a parent moves out, is the price we pay for loving and is the most natural thing in the world. As such, feeling upset and angry is highly desirable. There can be a tendency nowadays to want to move on as quickly as possible and not to be seen as weak or frail by expressing how we feel. While there can be some merit in having 'a stiff upper lip', we nevertheless feel what we feel and it is far better to express, in a controlled way, how we do feel rather than bury it and store up problems for the future.

Again it must be acknowledged that, as with adults, children are not a homogenous group and it may well be the case that each child in the family views things differently. One child may feel very upset and angry that dad has moved out, while another may not be at all distressed, may even feel relieved, having perhaps aligned themselves much more with the parent who is staying.

As well as this, any particular child, or indeed adult, may feel calm and relaxed about the situation at one time, to find themselves at other times absolutely overwhelmed by rage and upset, then calm again, and then angry and upset. These up-and-down emotional responses are a perfectly normal reaction and need to be recognised as such. For parents, it is particularly important to understand that if a child has been angry, and then ceases to be angry and becomes calm again, this does not mean that their trauma has been overcome once and for all. It is highly likely that these emotions will be revisited on several occasions by both parents and children. What will happen is that, over time, the gaps between these angry periods extend, and when they do occur they are less severe. With reasonable expression of those negative emotions, the individual eventually achieves some sense of normality again.

Disengaging

Tied in with this healing process, recovering from the pain of accepting the reality of the situation, is the next step of the process, which is disengagement from that relationship.

We can see this more easily for the parents involved in this situation. Initially, the parent who remains behind may feel outraged and angry at the parent who has left. They may wish the relationship to continue and seek to maintain that relationship at all costs. Over time, as the reality of the situation becomes apparent and they feel the upset that goes with that, they begin the process of disengaging from that individual and that relationship. As they progress, they develop some sense of their own resilience and the anger and distress can recede.

This is a rather more complex process for the children of the family as, of course, the fact that dad or mum has moved out of the family home does not necessarily mean that the relationship has gone. However, what would be expected to happen is that a child undergoes some 'letting go' of that parent so that, although the absent parent is no longer available on a day-to-day or week-to-week basis, the child learns to enjoy contact directly, or via telephone calls or other indirect means, and that parent remains a very important person in the child's life.

This can be a very difficult time for a youngster to manage and, indeed, it is difficult for parents to help their children through it. Parents have to take into account that children are often upset and hurt and what they say does not necessarily reflect their true feelings. For example, it is not at all unusual to hear a child say of an absent parent, even one with whom they had had a good relationship, 'I'm not bothered that he/she has gone. I don't mind.' This of course is recognised as a way of the child protecting themselves from the pain that they would be likely to feel if they fully acknowledged that they missed that loved parent very much indeed, and that it hurts like heck. On the other hand, a child saying that they are not bothered a parent has gone when there has never been a good relationship between that parent and that child, perhaps suggests that the child has moved on fairly rapidly and is not particularly traumatised by the parent leaving.

Parents know their children better than anyone else does and, by thinking about what the child is saying in relation to the history of the matter, a parent can make a reasonable distinction between these two scenarios. In the first scenario, the parent's job will be to help the child recognise that they do miss mum or dad and give permission for that grief and upset. In the second scenario the statement can be taken at face value and no action is necessary.

Establishing new relationships

Having moved through the first three parts of this process, the time comes when the parents and children are able to reinvest in other relationships.

For some adults this can be a fairly straightforward matter of developing a relationship with a new partner and building some sort of life together. Of course, the time it takes to reach this stage can vary tremendously, with some individuals moving on quite quickly and readily into new relationships while others take time, perhaps because their circumstances do not immediately afford them the opportunity to make new associations or they hold back in the belief that this will prevent their being hurt.

It should be mentioned that some individuals may never feel comfortable about moving into a new partnership because of the trauma they have experienced, or they may indeed find that they are perfectly contented alone and do no seek any permanent relationship but instead develop alternative kinds of relationships.

For the children of the family, reinvesting in other relationships depends to a large extent on the quality of the relationship they have retained with the absent parent. For example, if the child has a good relationship with an absent father, and mum moves on to a new relationship, it can be quite difficult for the youngster to accept mum's new partner and allow a good and positive relationship to develop with this new member of the family. On the other hand, a child whose absent father has not maintained a good relationship with the child or who has, indeed, absented himself completely from the child's life may have made it somewhat easier for the child to engage with mum's new partner.

At times children need to be given permission to develop new relationships. An absent parent can be very helpful in this regard; but if they suggest to the child, by word or deed, that it is not good to engage in this new relationship, then clearly they are placing the child in a very difficult position indeed. While one can understand that separated parents have their own needs, thoughts and feelings on such matters, this book is more concerned with the needs of the children, and, if at all possible, it is far better that the absent parent permits the child to consider entering into a new relationship. Hopefully, it will be recognised that, even if the new partner is a good person who will work with the remaining parent in providing day-to-day care for the child, a parent will always be a parent even if no longer living with the family. Anything that seeks to argue against this is certainly not in the child's best interest.

On the other hand, a new partner in the family who seeks to take over the parenting role may experience resentments and upset that the child could feel under those circumstances. The message for the new partner of the remaining parent is to make themselves as available, warm and helpful to the child as possible, and to wait for the child to come to them in terms of developing an emotional relationship.

The parent who remains caring for the children needs to be very careful here and recognise that, while they may have moved on from the children's other parent, the children may not have done so. While the children might be pleased that mum has a new partner, he cannot be a substitute for the absent parent, even if his relationship with the children develops some parenting qualities. In addition, although a parent may be in the exciting throes of a new relationship with someone they may care a great deal for and in time come to love, they cannot reasonably expect the children to feel exactly the same as they do about this new partner. A mismatch between the parents and the children can be a source of distress and discomfort for all concerned.

Advances and setbacks

The grieving process is often presented as a linear progression of accepting the reality of the loss, feeling the pain, disengaging, and then reinvesting in other relationships. However, real life is rarely as simple as that and, far from going smoothly through steps 1, 2, 3 and 4, it is often the case that individuals move backwards and forwards through this process, at times failing to accept that the relationship is over and at others appearing to have come to terms with that fact. They can find themselves particularly surprised, as can those around them, when suddenly they have seemed to have 'lost' that reality again and believe the relationship can be resurrected.

Nevertheless, for the vast majority of people, whatever the length of time it has taken and whether the journey has been gentle or traumatic, the desired destination is reached. They realise that the relationship is over or that it will be maintained in different circumstances, they have accepted that this is upsetting, but nevertheless they can move on in their lives. Each parent may develop a new relationship: the children can accept this and are allowed to form a bond with new partners.

What children often say during this phase

Will mummy and daddy get back together?

This is perhaps the most understandable and expected question, and is often put by children who are still at stage one of the process in that they are not able to understand or accept the reality of the situation that the absent parent has gone, and gone for good.

Accepting the reality is difficult but it needs to be reinforced by both parents, with massive reassurance that the children are still loved and will be cared for.

Why do people get angry with me when I'm upset?

A child going through the second stage, who is feeling the pain of the reality of the loss, can be very angry and upset. Parents and siblings may be deeply immersed in their own distress and, in such circumstances, are remote from what another family member is feeling. They may also feel generally hopeless and helpless and unable to deal with the situation.

Recognise that, though it may be impossible to find the right reassuring words, the child needs to be cuddled and comforted despite being angry, upset and perhaps difficult to get close to.

No one is listening to me. Doesn't anyone care what I feel?

I think it the most understandable thing in the world for a parent going through the trauma of divorce, and feeling the consequent upset and distress, not to pick up on a child's upset and distress for a time. Children often feel that they are not being listened to, or not heard or recognised, in this sort of situation. Thankfully, most parents, even during the course of upset, remain at some level tuned into their children or, more reasonably, once their upset lessens, can once again quickly pick up on the needs of the children.

It is perfectly acceptable for parents not to meet their children's needs every minute of every day, particularly when they are themselves very disturbed. Nevertheless, knowing that the children are likely to be distressed hopefully means that the parent will tune into the children's upset and, even if they can't deal with it at that precise moment because of their own problems, hopefully at the earliest opportunity they will be able to listen to their children and attend to their needs.

I am getting used to the way things are now. Does that mean I don't love dad so much any more?

Over time, as indicated above, children do come to understand the reality of the situation and the upset they feel does begin to diminish. Although this is a very welcome state of affairs it can, of itself, bring difficulty in that the child may feel disloyal to the absent parent.

Again the child needs lots of reassurance from the absent parent, and permission to feel what he or she does feel. Tell the child that though they are moving on and the deepest trauma has probably passed, it doesn't mean that they don't love mum or dad any more. They need to understand that being able to develop a life without the absent parent there all the time is the desired outcome.

Sometimes mum seems fine but then she gets upset all over again.

This is a situation that can be very confusing for parents who had thought 'Well, I'm okay now', then they suddenly find themselves upset all over again.

This statement simply reflects the child's equal level of confusion. All concerned simply need to rally round and acknowledge how awful the situation is, and reflect on the fact that, at times, they all feel okay and at other times they feel less okay but that gradually things will improve.

Some days I am okay but then I get upset again.

This statement from a child simply reinforces what we have said in the previous point, except that on this occasion the child has recognised for him or herself that moods, thoughts and feelings about the situation can go up and down.

As above, the child needs to be reassured that they are not alone in having see-sawing emotions and, however awful things seem at times, they will get better.

Sometimes it just hurts so much.

Parents are often aware of how deeply adults can feel at the breakdown of a relationship. They might not be realise that it can be amazingly hurtful for children too.

Even if in the throes of their own distress, parents need to find the time, effort and energy to allow the children to explore their thoughts and feelings. Those feelings need to be legitimised and recognised as being real and painful. There may be no words of comfort that can be offered, but cuddles and reassurance are still the best tools that we can use.

Sometimes I think dad is right and other times I think mum is.

Even if they realise that it is the parents' job to sort out the adult stuff, children can nevertheless strive to make sense of a situation in whatever way they can. Like the adults involved in the situation, they may seek to take sides and to see dad or mum as the person who is in the right or in the wrong.

Parents need to rise above their own thoughts and feelings on this matter and simply remind the children that these are grown up things, while it is the children's job to maintain their relationship with both parents. This is easy to write down but incredibly difficult to do, particularly if one is in the throes of a particularly angry, upset phase when the other parent is viewed very negatively indeed. However, sometimes we have to put our own emotions to one side for the benefit of our children. If we simply gave in to our raw feelings, without thought to how these are impacting on the children, then I am afraid we would have to say we were not doing the best by the children.

It is inevitable that there will be phases when a parent loses control and is not able to put the children's needs to the fore. However, providing these are very short lived and the parent is able to quickly pick up on these issues in a more reasonable manner, the children will not suffer unduly. Genuine difficulties will, however, arise if these issues are not dealt with for too long and the children are simply left to dwell on issues that they are ill equipped to deal with or that it would be impossible for them to resolve.

How can I still love them both?

This is related to the previous question, in that a child may perfectly reasonably still love his mum and dad, even having seen them shouting and yelling and generally being hateful to one another.

It would be unreasonable to expect parents to ignore their antagonism, but they should certainly try to amend their behaviour in front of the children and they should both reassure the children that they are still loved by both parents, even though they are upset and angry.

I miss dad all the time. It's just awful.

Here we have a child who is either at the early days of separation or who has still not understood and adjusted to the reality of the situation. The child has not lessened his or her strong emotional investment in the father.

While maintaining such strong emotions towards an absent parent can be viewed as a positive thing, nevertheless, for the child's own well-being there needs to be help to recognise that dad has gone and will not be returning to the family, and the child needs to find some way of slightly disengaging from dad to ease the constant suffering.

This may require action from both parents. They need, as calmly as possible, to reinforce the reality that mum and dad will not be getting back together, but that both mum and dad continue to love the child. Dad, in this case in particular, needs to give permission to the child to let go a little and move on. This can be very painful for both the parent and the child: mum needs to support the child through this and recognise the source of the potential upset and anger displayed by the child at this time.

I'm getting used to seeing dad at contact. It's lovely to see him but it's sad when it's over.

In a sense this is one stage moved on from the previous statement whereby it is clear that the child has maintained a good relationship with the absent parent and is able to enjoy time spent with him or her, even if it is sad when that time is over. This child seems to have moved further through the process and has disengaged slightly from dad such that he can function on a day-to-day basis but still retain enough relationship with dad that he enjoys spending time with him.

It is likely that no action need be taken by the parents at this time, as the child appears to be passing through the grieving process in a perfectly reasonable manner.

My brother is letting me down by wanting to be with dad.

This statement supports what we recognised earlier, that different people have different relationships and move through the grieving process at different times. It may be the case that a child who is particularly upset at dad leaving, because of the closeness of their relationship or because they were aware of the distress caused to the parent who stayed behind, may feel very hurt and upset at a sibling who has either has accepted the situation for what it is and is coping with the changed circumstances of the relationship, or is enjoying a relationship with the absent parent that they never had when that parent was at home.

A child with these thoughts and feelings needs help and support, including being helped to understand that, at some time in the future, they may feel better in themselves and able to resume the relationship they had with the absent parent, or even to improve upon it. They may also need help to recognise that the strong feelings they have at the moment may not be shared by a sibling. The sibling may have felt like that in the past or, indeed, may feel like that in the future, but at the moment they are very happy seeing dad. It is hoped that the child could gain some understanding, in an age-appropriate manner, as to how matters are progressing, not just for themselves but for other people too.

I'm not sure how I should be feeling about my mum's/dad's new partner.

There are lots of issues around the establishing of new relationships, whether it is the absent parent or the remaining parent who has a new partner. I intend to deal more fully with this subject in Chapter Six, but for now I am simply flagging up that moving from the third into the fourth phase of the grieving process and developing new relationships can have both positive and negative connotations for all the family members.

Tasks for Parents During the Moving On Phase

1. Acknowledge your own feelings

Moving on from a broken relationship can be very difficult indeed and is recognised as being akin to, and indeed more complex than, grieving over a death. It is only to be expected that the adults involved will be feeling very upset, and fearful about their future.

The first task for parents at this time is to recognise their own feelings and thoughts on the matter and how this is impacting on themselves, let alone the children.

2. Be aware of your child's feelings

However, parents are still charged with the responsibility of caring for their children, so at time they must strive to put their own distress slightly to one side to enable them to stay tuned into their children's feelings.

3. Be aware of the difference between your own and your children's feelings

A parent is likely to be moving on once and for all from the relationship with their former partner. The children will be going through a different process, taking on board fundamental change within the family. At this time children are likely to say things or behave in such a manner that it is obvious that they are angry, confused, disappointed or whatever.

Parents should recognise that each child will have his or her own feelings and may be out of step with the progress being made by other family members. Parents should remain as cool, calm and collected as possible, to help the child recognise their distress and then ventilate it in an appropriate manner.

4. Do not encourage your child to take sides

The desired outcome is for children to maintain a good and positive relationship with both parents. It is, therefore, incumbent upon each parent to discourage the children from taking sides in any disputes and to give them permission to be on good terms with the other parent.

5. Give your child permission to be upset

One of the big tasks for parents during this phase is to give their children permission to be upset and also to find ways to help them take back some of the very powerful emotions they may have about the absent parent in particular. Even if those emotions are positive, it is perfectly possible that the strength of the relationship is actually causing a child grief, which could be dealt with by a lessening of that attachment.

This does not mean letting go of the absent parent altogether. It simply recognises that a child cannot maintain that level of attachment if a parent is not to be in their lives on a day-to-day basis. This should never be allowed to go too far the other way, where a child is encouraged to discontinue their attachment to the absent parent.

Summary

Following the breakdown of the marriage or relationship and one parent leaving, all members of the family, not least the children, will need to adjust to the new circumstances of their lives. This must be undertaken, though each individual will take his or her own time to go through the process. Being aware of this, and accepting that your emotions may not be matched by what others are feeling at a particular time, will be of great value in ensuring that the adults and children involved survive emotionally intact following this time of great change.

Human beings are incredibly resilient and, with a reasonable amount of love and support, most families find themselves at the end of the process without having needed professional help. Sometimes families or individuals would benefit from external assistance and this will be discussed in the second half of this book.

CHAPTER 5

Changing Lifestyles, Changing Roles

As we have seen, the ending of the parents' relationship and the break-up of a family leads to many changes. In this chapter I wish to highlight two facets of that change – change of lifestyle and change of roles for both parents and children.

Financial repercussions

A relationship ending will often have a significant impact on family finances. It may be the case that the parents must now maintain two homes, the absent parent having moved into new accommodation or perhaps sharing with someone to whom they make a financial contribution. It may be necessary to sell up the former family home, which could result in moving away from a familiar area and the children having to change school. At a lesser extreme it may be that the absent parent has gone off with the family car, leaving the family to rely on public transport, or simply that the family finds that there is not the money available that was enjoyed previously.

Some of these issues may appear comparatively trivial to the parents but for the children concerned they can be very serious indeed. Although children can be fickle creatures at times, they tend not to like any change and, if deprived of the things they enjoy, such as treats that rely on money – sweets, family days out, visits to the cinema, easy access to other activities – they can become very dejected and unhappy. We have to be aware that some of the upset and anger experienced by the children, as well as by the parents of course, is because of this deprivation in addition to the loss of a family member.

Of course, moving house, moving area, leaving a familiar school and starting at another, are all very significant for children. Not only do they lose the bricks and mortar of the family home, but it is likely they will also have to move away from established friendships. They will have go through grieving processes for these other relationships as well, not just the significant family relationships.

The children's education

Moving to a new area frequently means changing school which, for children of any age, can be very difficult even though schools bend over backwards to accommodate the needs of new children, particularly when they are aware of potentially traumatic family circumstances.

However, a move to a new school is not simply about making friends in a strange environment, important though that is. Most state schools follow the national curriculum, but teaching methods and the passage through the curriculum by different schools will vary and the new children may struggle academically for some time, finding themselves at odds with the other pupils. The emotional and behavioural repercussions of integrating into a new school can find their expression in disharmony at home. Both the remaining and the absent parent may find themselves bearing the brunt of angry exchanges resulting from their children's upset at these and other factors.

Parents should develop a good dialogue with the school. Teachers and other staff are invariably child centred – that is their job – and they will be concerned to ensure that the child is supported not only academically but also socially and emotionally.

Role extension and reduction

Even nowadays, it is rare for both parents to have equal responsibility for and expertise in all the many aspects of child care and household management. In most families there will have evolved individual areas of family life that the mother or the father usually fulfils, whether that has come about for practical reasons or because one parent was more able or willing to undertake a particular activity than the other. The children of the family will have become familiar with these demarcations so that they will tend to go to one parent with, say, a grazed knee or a letter from the school and to the other with a broken toy or frozen computer keyboard.

After parents separate, each will probably have to undertake roles that previously the other parent carried out. This might be obvious in the case of the remaining parent, but to some extent it can also apply to the absent parent at times of contact. From a positive point of view, both parents could see this as an opportunity to enjoy aspects of parenthood that they hadn't participated in before. However, it is likely that the parents will be overwhelmed at times by the sheer practicality of attempting to fulful the children's needs without the backup of a second responsible adult. They might also have to learn about aspects of care for their children with which they previously had little involvement.

Equally, a parent might find that they have to hand over to the other an activity that was previously seen by the adult and the child as special time for the two of them. It is also possible that a parent will be anxious during times of contact, for instance, that their ex-partner is not providing the same level of care for the children that they receive at home.

For the parents, having to take on or hand over family responsibilities can cause its own resentments and distress. For the child it is a further reminder of the family's change of circumstances. It may initially be confusing and worrying for them as they learn to accept and trust their parents in new roles. Clearly this is another area where communication between the parents is vital for the well-being of themselves and the children.

Role reversal

It is not at all unusual to find that a child appears to be coping with the breakdown of the marriage and a parent moving out better than the parent who is left behind. It may well be the case that, because of their own particular emotional distress, parents are no longer functioning in that role and for a while a child is expected to 'look after' the parent. An older child especially may find themselves acting as confidante and supporter of a parent rather than the other way around. Younger children may also find themselves in this situation too, but they are obviously less well equipped to deal with it.

Parents need to take account of the fact that they may become very emotionally needy and, while it is nice to have cuddles with one's children at a time of upset, it is really support from other adults that will benefit the adult, while relieving the child of a burden that they are simply not equipped to deal with. Hopefully this will be a short-lived period, and mum or dad will soon find they are in a state of mind to take control of the situation again.

Attitudes to family breakdown

Although divorce and separation have become commonplace, sadly there still seems to be a degree of negativity regarding family breakdown. The parents themselves may find it difficult to share with family and friends that their relationship has come to an end, that they have in some way 'failed', and that their partner has moved out and is setting up home elsewhere. Similarly, children, too, can find it very difficult to confide in family, friends or school about the change in their family circumstances.

It is particularly important for parents to ensure that the school is fully informed, within levels of appropriate confidentiality, of the circumstances of the family so the school can assist the child through this potentially very difficult phase.

Children's views on sexuality

This is an issue that people frequently shy away from, but it is nevertheless one that I feel should be addressed as, following a split, children can be faced fully head on with their parents' sexuality.

Children in general seldom recognise their parents as sexual beings. Young children, of course, have no knowledge of such matters. Later on, though they may become aware of 'the facts of life' to a greater or lesser degree, they may still find it difficult, even undesirable, to relate what they know to their own parents. By the time of adolescence, when children are coming to terms with their own sexual potential, they often find it impossible to contemplate that their parents have ever felt, let alone still feel, very much the same way. One often hears children of all ages laughing or being embarrassed about parents kissing, cuddling or whatever.

When a parent begins a new relationship a child is faced with the potentially difficult transformation of boring or conventional mum or dad suddenly becoming someone quite unknown to them – someone else's boyfriend or girlfriend. Of course, it may well be the case that the parent who left did so because they already had a new partner, in which case it is highly likely that the absent partner's sexuality has been made perfectly clear by the remaining parent, often in very colourful and graphic language.

However, one of the positive aspects of parents starting new relationships and the child having to confront a parent's sexuality is that this development can be of enormous benefit to the parent, perhaps after a period when all seemed gloom and doom. The knock-on effect for the child is that they find themselves with a parent who is happy again, rather than miserable.

What Children Often Say During This Phase

Where am I going to live?

This is, of course, a fairly fundamental question that simply reflects the uncertainty under which the family may be living. Even if the child ultimately continues to live within the family home, there may have been a time when it was not clear that remaining there was viable. If this anxiety percolates through to the children, it may be very difficult indeed for the parent to reassure the child adequately.

Many of the family issues need to remain adult issues and we should try to protect children from things they simply do not need to know. However, in reality, if one is very upset and anxious it is almost impossible to prevent children being aware of that. As many reassurances that can be reasonably given should be given, though they must be rooted in reality. If it is in fact likely that the family will be moving home, with the consequent wider disruptions that go with that, then children do need to be told that, but not before they have asked. It is not necessary to burden children with information about the many options the parents are discussing while arrangements are still very much up in the air.

Children need to prepare themselves for these moves, just as they had to when the relationship broke down and one parent left home, and with ongoing support they will make these moves with some trauma, but will come out the other end perfectly well.

Where will I spend Christmas?

Although this sounds trivial, it simply reflects the fact that such questions did not need to be asked when the parents were living together. Now that the parents are apart, at significant times such as birthdays, Christmas and other festivals throughout the year, decisions will have to be made about who will have whom, where the child will be spending time, and how that time will be shared out.

As I have said many times throughout this book, parents are parents forever: no matter what their feelings are to one another, they still have to work together for the benefit of the children. Parents need to be planning for all of these issues well in advance so that children are presented with their parents' joint plan and they are spared confusion and worry. It might also be that you both feel that, in an age-appropriate way, the children themselves can participate in making arrangements and express some preferences.

Will I have to change school?

Children will become aware that the family circumstances have changed significantly and that their parents are considering living and educational arrangements.

Parents, jointly, need to give very careful thought to this because, although the family may indeed be moving home, it may be possible for the child to continue to attend their school. The importance of this is not only continuity in the curriculum but of course also the continuity in friendships and other adult relationships that the child has developed. These school-related associations can prove very helpful to children and provide an oasis of stability in a world that seems to be shifting around them.

However, if the child does have to change school, this needs to be faced head on and carefully planned for. Incorporating the child into that planning can be very helpful and allows the child to retain a feeling of control rather than simply being managed.

Why can't we go on holiday any more?

This often reflects the changed financial circumstances in which the family finds itself. With the family perhaps financing two households, money can become tight and areas such as holidays and other social events may be so altered that the child notices a change for the worse.

This might appear to be a fairly trivial issue in the midst of all the other changed circumstances, but to the children it may be very important. I am not suggesting that children are wholly mercenary by any means, but it is often these areas of obvious financial constraint that can really bring it home to the child that things have radically altered and that, perhaps, the world is never going to be quite the same again.

Children can be told that mummy or daddy has to be more careful how they spend their money now. The family will be okay but the children cannot have the all treats they enjoyed previously. This has to be reality based but should not be presented in a way that could generate anxiety in the child. It is recognised that this is a difficult job for parents, particularly if they are themselves worried about the future.

It's dad's fault we had to sell the house.

This is another of the issues that can lead to very significant difficulty if not dealt with sensitively. If dad has left and the home has had to be sold, then this can be a tangible example of something on which we can vent our anger, children included. In these circumstances, one can see that it is very easy for the absent parent to be blamed for the need to sell the house or for not being able to afford activities that the children had enjoyed. Of course, as adults we understand that it takes two to make a marriage and very often two to break one, and, although one parent leaves, it may not be the case that he or she is wholly to blame.

One or other of the parents may find themselves suggesting, against their better judgement, that it is all the other parent's fault. Hard as it is, especially if they feel very, very angry indeed towards the absent parent, the remaining parent must recognise that it is in no one's interest to allow the children to turn the absent parent into the villain of the piece. So, without laying blame anywhere, they must explain to the children that it is just the circumstances of the breakdown that have led to such a radical necessity as having to move home.

It's nice when I see dad. He doesn't shout or get upset like you do.

The parent left behind may indeed be very angry or depressed and sometimes on a short fuse temperamentally, while the parent who has left the family home may be feeling fairly happy about the situation. I think it is perfectly reasonable for a child to notice that time spent with a parent in buoyant mood is a nice escape from a household where things are not as settled and happy. For the remaining parent this can be extremely upsetting: not only has their ex-partner given them a raw deal in leaving them and breaking up the family, but now seems to be rubbing their nose in it by providing their children with happiness and fun when they are feeling particularly awful.

Both parents have a role here. Whilst sympathising with and understanding the child, nevertheless they have to encourage some understanding in the child of the other parent's distress. The parent who has left still has the job of supporting the other parent in his or her care for the child, including if necessary explaining to the child why it is that mum or dad is so upset.

Dad's taken the car. We can't go anywhere.

Again, this is a reflection that the children are recognising a tangible change in their lives where they no longer have easy access to a car to take them around. They might find themselves in that awful position of having to rely on public transport!

The serious side of this is that often the more deep-seated emotions that the children feel about the breakdown of the family, and the loss of a loved parent, may come to the fore with this very tangible example of change in their lives.

Both parents have to recognise that, although this may appear a trivial complaint, it can be used as a discussion point to help the child explore, and ventilate, their feelings about the separation.

I've got to look after my mum/dad. They're not coping at all.

Children can be very astute and will often recognise that their mum or dad is not coping when they see them upset and tearful. While eventually children may get angry about this, at the beginning their sensitive nature often comes to the fore and they find themselves wanting to care for the upset parent.

This is all well and good if the child is equipped to deal with this to a greater or lesser extent but, of course, many children are not. As indicated earlier, adult family and friends are very important to have around at this time to relieve the children of this burden.

Tasks for Parents During this Phase of Change

1. Anticipate and deal with problems

The break up of the family will lead to changes in roles for its members, as well as changes in family lifestyle. Parents need to consider and anticipate the impact upon the whole family, particularly the children.

While it is inevitable that some upset and distress will be exhibited by the children, parents need to re-establish their role as parents without delay, even though they may be living separately, to ensure that their children's lives are stabilised as quickly as possible.

2. Do not rely on your children for emotional support

Particularly during the early stages, it is anticipated that parents will be upset and distressed and may not be able to fulfil their traditional role as parents of their children. It may well be the case that, for a while, the children take over this role and are caring for – in effect parenting – their parents.

While the love and care of one's children is to be welcomed and can be a great source of comfort, most children are not equipped to carry out this task for lengthy periods, and, as such, it is incumbent upon parents to ensure that their emotional needs are met elsewhere. Parents should talk to their own friends and families if they feel the need for emotional support.

3. Seek support from others outside the immediate family

Parents must recognise that in future their children will, by definition, be functioning as part of a one-parent family. While this of itself need not be to the ultimate detriment of the children, they will nevertheless need help during the transition. In particular, it is important to liaise with their school and with family and friends who are able to support the children through this significant change in their lives.

In addition, although one-parent families are quite commonplace nowadays, children can still feel very upset and embarrassed when having to explain to others that mum or dad has left home.

4. Deal with the impact of financial constraints

In the vast majority of cases, family breakdown and the separation of parents will have a negative effect on family finances. At the extreme this may involve selling the family home, and the children and the remaining parent moving to a smaller home or perhaps into a less desirable area. However, less extreme factors such as loss of the family car or other financial constraints may provide tangible examples to the children that their life is changed forever.

While children may have some difficulty in expressing their strong feelings about deep-seated emotional problems regarding the family breakdown and, perhaps, the loss of a parent, these smaller-scale changes can be the triggers for far more easily vocalised strong reactions on their part. As has been suggested above, these complaints can be useful inroads for exploring the child's feelings on more serious matters.

5. Keep in contact with the children's school

Schools are very adept at supporting children but they do need to be informed of individual family circumstances. When children move to a new school, they may find the disruption in their education and social relationships difficult to manage. They may struggle academically for a time as they adjust to different teaching styles and the school's approach to the curriculum.

It may be that for a while one or both of the parents have to increase the amount of help that up to now they have given their children with their homework. It is worth a little extra input in this area if it prevents the children finding themselves behind others in the class or having difficulty with a subject that they previously found easy, which would only add to the problems they are already having to cope with. This is another reason why good communication with the school is essential: any parent will know how much primary and secondary education has changed since their own schooldays, so you need to know that you are helping them in the correct and up-to-date way.

Summary

I think the overall comment to make at this time is that changing roles and lifestyles simply reflect that the family is in a state of flux. For a while it may be uncertain where people are going to be living and with whom they are going to be living. They may be uncertain whether the family will remain financially viable. There may be moves of house or school, and moving away from friends and having to make new friends, which can be destabilising for all concerned but particularly so for the children.

Although relationships and living arrangements within the family may have changed fundamentally, it is important to allow the children to establish a new way of living, to develop new routines and new relationships as quickly as possible and for any disruption to be kept to the minimum.

It is recognised that this will be undertaken at a time when the parent or parents are probably feeling less able to fulfil the parenting role than they ever have before. However, as is stressed throughout this book, the emphasis is on the needs of the child and, therefore, parents must at times put their own emotions and inner turmoil on hold in order to carefully consider and put into action what is best for the child.

CHAPTER 6

New Families

Once separation has taken place and everyone involved is learning to adjust to the new circumstances, children often find themselves in new family situations. This is, of course, an extremely sensitive time and needs careful handling.

Anticipating the difficulties

For the adults, however well they have managed the split up to this point, recognising that one's partner has now moved on to a new relationship can add a new dimension of anger and hostility. While the parent providing day-to-day care for the child may have been perfectly supportive of the notion of the child of the family going off to have contact with the absent parent, that may suddenly come into question when the child reports that they are not only seeing mum or dad but are also meeting with mum or dad's partner. Obviously, finding out through the children is not the best way to receive this news and ongoing communication is imperative if the children are to be spared from being caught up in these very difficult circumstances. In any case, each parent should keep the other informed, at a reasonable level, about the children's activities in their home and during contact, which includes when you wish to introduce them to a new partner.

Children's feelings about a new partner

It is not at all unusual to hear a child say that they have met mum or dad's new partner and that they don't like them very much. However, on closer inspection it may well be the case that the child has got on very well indeed with that person but realises that it may not be the most sensitive thing in the world to go home and tell mum or dad how nice they are. If the parents have not given their children permission to move on and begin to enjoy these new relationships, the children will seek to manage it somehow, even if it means they try to negate their own positive feelings about this new person in their life.

However, when children say that they do not like mum or dad's new partner, we also have to take into account that this may be true. One cannot like everyone in this life and there may be something about the new partner that genuinely makes the child uncomfortable.

Both parents, but obviously the parent with the new partner in particular, must ensure that they give the child every opportunity to express his or her reasons for being reluctant to connect with the new partner. The parents must then consider very carefully whether, in the light of what the child says, the child may eventually feel able to form a good relationship with this new adult and that this is, indeed, desirable, or whether the child's feelings are unlikely ever to change. In the latter case, the parent may have to ensure that contact with the child excludes the new partner.

A new partner's attitude to the children

However, we also have to take into account the fact that a new partner may very much welcome the new relationship but doesn't particularly like the fact that their new love has a family already. He or she may well attempt to put up barriers to ongoing relationships between the parent and the children. This situation, in which the new partner is in effect thinking 'I want your dad but I don't want his children' or 'I want your mum but I don't want her children', has for a long time been recognised as the wicked stepmother (or stepfather) syndrome.

Step-siblings

A complicating feature in the lives of the children is if the absent parent has formed a relationship with a new partner who already has children.

By leaving the family home, the absent parent has already demonstrated to the children that they find it acceptable to no longer be with them on a day-to-day basis. At the same time, it is to be hoped that the children have been reassured that the contact arrangements that have been made will enable them to maintain a loving and caring relationship. It is not surprising, then, if a child is confused and hurt to realise that the parent is spending a great deal of time with other children and, perhaps, only a few hours a week with his or her own. In this situation, the child is likely to be thinking 'Why did he leave me behind when he's off with them?' and 'Does he love her children more than he loves me?'.

One also often hears children say that the new partner prefers their own children. This may indeed be true and only natural, which in some respects could make it easier for the absent parent to reinforce that they will always be the child's parent and will love them above any other person's children. Above all, the child should be made to feel a welcome and equal member of the household during the time that he or she is there.

New relationships finalise the break

It is not at all unusual for children over weeks, months or even years to still carry within them somewhere the hope that mum and dad will get back together again and they can return to being a 'normal' family. Watching their mum and dad moving into new relationships brings a further finality to the fact that mum and dad do not love each other any more and there is unlikely to be reconciliation.

Although some children might see mum or dad having a new partner as a positive development, we also have to accept that sadly, for many children, it can be a negative experience. It may simply be the situation that mum or dad is very overwhelmed with the enormity of their new relationship, enjoying very much being the new boyfriend or girlfriend and, for a while, the child may feel that this new partner has replaced themselves as the foremost person in their mum's or dad's affection.

What Children Often Say During this Phase

Daddy's got a new girlfriend and now mummy is upset again.

The breakdown of relationships is bad enough, but watching a partner move on into new relationships can be particularly difficult. Adults who thought they were coping with the breakdown of their marriage reasonably well can find themselves revisiting earlier trauma and upset. In addition, the children of the family may meet this new partner during contact and come back reporting that they had a wonderful time.

They may of course come back saying they had an awful time. This might indeed be the case, but it is also possible that they did enjoy themselves but realise it would be insensitive to say as much. The parents must continue to liaise about how things are and maintain a reasonable rapport, even though they might feel upset and angry with one another, so that the children can be helped to recognise that it is okay to like these new people, even if mummy or daddy doesn't.

Why does mummy keep changing her boyfriends?

I think this indicates the need to protect children from transient relationships.

It is unlikely that a single parent wishing ultimately to form a new permanent partnership will hit on the right person straight away and there may well be a period when the parent is venturing into a new social life and getting to know several people. Enjoying the freedoms and possibilities of the single life might be fine, but it is not particularly helpful to the stability of the children if they are introduced to a succession of 'aunts' and 'uncles'.

While it is right and proper that children meet with more or less permanent partners of their mum or dad, the parent concerned must first get to know a person very well in order to assess his or her suitability to enter into the family life. Having said that, it should also be remembered that, particularly following instability in their lives, children will want to know where their parents are going when they go out, and who with. The parent should judge just how much children need to be told so that they do not worry about the parent, and equally so they do not begin to speculate prematurely about the possibility of a new adult entering into their lives.

Dad's girlfriend doesn't like me.

This may be an accurate assessment; a new partner may like dad or mum very much but not care for dad or mum's children. On the other hand it may be the case that the child has judged too soon and that, over time and as relationships develop, the new partner comes to play an important role in the child's life. One would be very surprised indeed if warm and encouraging relationships were struck up at the first meeting.

All concerned need to recognise the need to go at a slow pace and that, although mum or dad may have developed very positive feelings for this new partner, the child cannot be expected to feel the same. Neither the child nor the new partner should be pressurised into expecting more of the relationship than can reasonably be expected. The parents should continue to liase with the each other to ensure that they know the conditions in which the child will be living and that the child is happy in them. This obviously applies during times of contact, but the permanent carer also needs to ensure that the absent parent is still aware of a child's circumstances particularly if there have been, or are about to be, any changes.

However, it is possible that a parent may face a terrible dilemma whereby they have this ongoing love for a child who cannot achieve a comfortable relationship with the new partner. At its extreme, the parent may have to choose between the child and the partner.

I don't like living with Uncle John and I want to go and live with my dad.

Following the breakdown of the marriage and dad or mum leaving the family home, a child may initially have been very contented to have stayed with the other parent. When a new partner comes along for the parent with whom they are living, this can be an extremely unwelcome change for the child.

As with the scenario above, this may be a short-lived phase and in time the new partner becomes a much loved member of the family. However, at the other extreme the child may simply be unable to cope with this new person in the family and express a wish to live with the absent parent instead, or, indeed, with the absent parent and their partner.

Again, it is important to recognise that this is an issue that needs to be handled with tremendous sensitivity and, while one would expect that the adults concerned remained focused on the best needs of the child, this can be a time of great stress within the family.

It's nice when I see dad but I feel awful about leaving mum.

This is a situation that must be anticipated instead of waiting until the child is obviously having difficulties concerned with divided loyalties and concern about leaving a parent they believe will decline in their absence. The child must be reassured from the very start that they have permission to go and have a nice time with the absent parent.

I don't like to tell mum I have had a nice time at dad's because I think she would be upset.

In essence this follows on from the above. If a child returns from contact and says they have not enjoyed it, it may well be the case that the child is protecting you from knowledge that they think will upset you and is telling you what they think you want to hear.

I am not suggesting, in any way, that this is a deliberate ploy on the part of the child but, again, one would recognise that this is a situation that should be anticipated as being fairly normal and the child needs to be given absolute permission not only to go and have a nice time but also to say as much when they return.

I hate going to see dad. I never liked him anyway.

This, of course, is the reverse of the above and simply recognises that, in the real world, not all relationships are ideal or even positive and it may well be the case that a particular child and their parent never got on well. This 'not good' relationship may be made even worse by the circumstances of the family breakdown and it may be quite legitimate for the child not to want to see the absent parent.

While one would expect that, initially, at the very least the child would be encouraged to see, and to try and maintain a relationship with, the absent parent, armed with the knowledge of the history of the situation it may be that this relationship is never going to improve and as such is not worth striving to preserve.

I get scared when I go to dad's. I hated it when he hit mum.

It's a sad fact that some children have seen dad hit mum, mum hit dad, or mum and dad having serious rows and difficulties. If the parents did indeed do wrong things to each other, it needs to be assessed whether either parent could ever pose a risk to the child.

I cannot give hard and fast advice on this here because every situation that might involve violence or abuse has to be assessed separately. This is, however, a significant issue that is looked at later in the book (see pages 132–3) but for now it needs to be recognised that, even in those families where violence did not occur but there were rows, the child may fear that there will be a continuance or even an escalation when he or she is alone with a parent.

It is very important that parents continue to liaise with one another to give the child every reassurance that he or she is perfectly reasonable in their worry and concern, but it was just a phase the family went through that is now over, and will not be an ongoing feature of any relationships within the family.

I think dad sees me just to quiz me about mum.

It is very difficult for some parents not to ask children about the other parent – what they are doing, who they are doing it with, and generally what they are up to in their life – especially if the parents are not communicating properly with each other.

Children can feel very uncomfortable indeed when they feel they are being quizzed about mum or dad, whether it is the parent with whom they are going to contact asking the question or, indeed, mum or dad asking questions on return from contact. While it may be perfectly acceptable to ask a child 'How's mum/dad today?', more than that is really not to be welcomed.

The common sense approach here is simply to make general enquiries and show an ongoing interest in the absent parent but, other than that, to recognise that it is not the children's job to relay mum or dad's activities.

Mum says I don't have to go and see dad so I think she'd prefer it if I didn't.

I think it is well recognised that it is important for a child to keep ongoing relationships with both parents and as such one would expect both parents to encourage contact. But a child who picks up on the sensitivities of one or both of the parents may seek to regulate his or her relationship with them in a way that avoids upsetting either parent. It is, of course, more often the case that the child is trying to interpret the feelings of the parent with whom they are living.

Saying 'If you want to go, you can, but if you don't then you don't have to' is not very helpful and I would much rather that parents said to their children, 'Yes, off you go. Have a nice time. I'll see you when you come back', rather than leave decisions to children at a time when they are ill-equipped to deal with them.

At its extreme, this sort of scenario can lead to the cessation of contact altogether, when really nobody wanted it to be like that.

I really worry about dad. Mum is happy now, but he isn't.

A statement like this can arise from the fact that separated parents move on in their lives at different speeds.

It may be the case that one parent is almost immediately happy to be relieved of the burden of a relationship they no longer wanted to be in, while the other is still feeling very unhappy about the situation. Again, the child may be concerned about this mismatch between the parents and try to take on the task of regulating the situation.

It is important that parents communicate properly to ensure that the children are not placed in this difficulty in the first place. However, if it does occur, the best that can be done is for both parents, whatever their own current state of mind or emotional situation, to reassure the children that they are as well as they can be at that time and they are not relying on the child to provide too much emotional support.

Yuk! They are all lovey-dovey. She wasn't like that with dad.

As mentioned before, as a result of the separation children can be confronted for the first time with the realisation that their parents are sexual beings. They are therefore likely to find overt signs of affection with a new partner, which they may not have witnessed between their parents when they were still together, unwelcome and embarrassing.

Starting a new relationship is exciting and the first flush of sexual excitement can be quite overwhelming. While on the one hand this is lovely and needs to be recognised as such, the parent and the new partner need to maintain a degree of sensitivity to ensure that they are behaving in the presence of the children in a way that they can cope with.

I went to meet his girlfriend and she was awful.

We have to take at least two possibilities into account here. The child may be saying what he or she actually thought, or may be saying what he or she thinks people want to hear. It will be necessary to ascertain which is really the case.

If the child genuinely doesn't like the new partner, as noted before, it may come to a choice between the partner and maintaining a relationship with the child. Another possibility would be to exclude the partner during contact between the parent and the child, but this is certainly not ideal, is unlikely to work for long, and is liable to cause friction and mistrust on all sides.

If, on the other hand, you know that the child got on perfectly well with dad's girlfriend but isn't saying so to avoid upsetting mum, once again the child needs to be given permission to enjoy this new person in their life and to be reminded that no relationship can diminish that between the mother and child.

I told mum that dad's girlfriend is nice and she went ballistic.

Going to see dad and meeting his new partner may have been a pleasant experience but the child is then placed in a very difficult position if mum lets it be known that she is displeased about there even being a girlfriend, that her child has met her, and on top of all that the child likes the girlfriend. It would be better if mum could show some magnanimity and say she is glad that the child has enjoyed being with dad and his new girlfriend, even if that is very far from what she is feeling. I do accept that this could be one of the hardest things to have to grit your teeth and do.

It would be hoped that, over time, the adult concerned could begin to deal with their own feelings in this matter and then genuinely be pleased that the child has this new and potentially rewarding relationship to enjoy.

Dad's girlfriend is okay but her kids are horrible/ Dad's girlfriend is okay but she likes her own kids more than me.

What the child tells the full-time caring parent when they return home may be real, or may not, and this again needs to be checked out between the adults concerned.

It might be that, though perfectly nice individuals, the children just don't get on well. In this case a child may not have the reasoning to understand this, or the vocabulary to express it; they are far more likely say and feel that these other children are just plain horrible. Parents, also, frequently bundle children together and tell them to play nicely; why they should expect this to happen, in the light of all the evidence of classmate rivalry and of siblings being at times at each other's throats, is baffling.

For some children, being thrust into a 'new family' is something they cope with perfectly well: others may need to go through a long process to develop relationships with potential new family members. Of course, parents know their own children best and need to remain sensitive to their needs and ensure those needs are met.

However, if it is the case that the child is distressed at contact, and actually not being made welcome by either dad's new partner or the new partner's children, then dad has to make it very clear where his priorities lies. If a good relationship cannot be developed between the child and the new partner and children, then it may well be the case that dad has contact on his own with his child and avoids the child coming into contact with these other individuals. A parent may have had high hopes of his own much loved child participating in a new relationship that is making him very happy and is likely to be saddened if this turns out to be impossible.

Tasks for Parents in New Relationships

1. Prepare for introducing your children to new partners

Many parents leave marital relationships to go off with someone else. Even if this is not the case, parents will inevitably begin to develop new relationships with other adults. It is anticipated that at some stage children will meet the new partners of their parents. This may happen very soon after the split, particularly when a parent have moved off to live with new partner, or it may happen some time later, after the children have settled into life in a single-parent home.

Therefore the first, and perhaps most important, task for parents during this time is to anticipate these new relationships, and begin to think through their own thoughts and feelings on this. Having to see a parent move off to live with another adult, or adult and children, can be very difficult for children, as can seeing the parent with whom they have day-to-day contact develop a new relationship. This difficulty does not need to be compounded by the children having to cope with their parents who are unprepared for the impact it will have on their own emotions.

2. Expect new relationships to upset adults

Although moving on to some form of new relationship is nearly always a positive step, parents who may now be coping reasonably well with the separation and divorce, and the moving away either of a partner or from a partner, can find themselves re-experiencing feelings of anger, upset and regret.

Focusing upon the needs of the children in this case, one would have to say that it is important, as far as possible, to put one's own thoughts and feelings on the matter to one side and allow the children to benefit as much as they can from these new relationships.

3. Don't expect your children to feel as you do

It must also be recognised that, though a parent may be developing a new relationship with someone to whom they feel very loving, it is not automatically the case that the child will relate well to that new adult, or, indeed, that the new adult will relate to the child. This can especially be the case if the new partner already has children from a previous relationship.

If a child very quickly develops a rapport with a new adult, or the adult with the child, then it is likely that that adult can be properly incorporated into contact. However, if a relationship does not develop easily, or there is any antagonism between the new adult and the child, the parent has to decide whether to maintain the relationship with the child or with the new adult. A compromise would be to arrange to see the child without the new adult (or their children, if applicable) being present, but this is not ideal and may well cause friction in the long term.

Recognise that it may take some time for such a relationship to develop and avoid pressurising either the new partner or the child in an attempt to speed things along. Insisting on incorporating a new adult into a child's life can be counterproductive and could result in the loss of relationship between a child and its parent, whether this is the absent parent or the parent who has the day-to-day care of the child.

4. Keep displays of affection in check

Overt public demonstrations of affection between two adults can be uncomfortable for onlookers at the best of times. For the children involved this can be unwelcome, disturbing and highly embarrassing.

A parent with a new partner should be sensitive to the children's feelings in this matter and ensure that their behaviour is kept at an appropriate level. They should also guard against their own positive feelings towards a new adult overwhelming their ability to recognise whether their child is happy with the new situation.

Summary

Entirely new issues will arise when new partners come on the scene. This can be a very painful experience for either the absent parent or the remaining parent, as they realise that their ex-partner has moved on to a new partner.

The children may also find this development upsetting and they need to be given permission to begin to engage in some degree of relationship or attachment to that new partner. This does not apply to transient partnerships; it would be counterproductive if, during a phase of meeting numerous 'aunts' and 'uncles', the child was encouraged to become attached to each possibly fleeting partner. What we are talking about here are those more meaningful relationships that develop between the adults and new partners, whom it is perfectly reasonable to expect the children to be introduced to and, indeed, to become part of their lives.

It should be recognised that reinvesting in relationships can be very difficult for children because, rather like their parents, they may be frightened of being hurt or disappointed again, and they may feel that forming a new attachment is in some way disloyal to their parents.

CHAPTER 7

Answers to Questions Often Asked by Parents

In this final chapter in Part One, I have drawn together questions that parents have asked when seeking assistance from either clinical or legal services. They are not presented in any particular order but are simply included here to flesh out some of the ideas and discussions that have been put forward in earlier chapters.

I feel really angry when I think about my ex. How can I keep these feelings under control?

Feeling angry and upset about one's ex-partner is not at all unusual and is part of the normal grieving process. One can well understand that, at times, these feelings of anger become very difficult to deal with.

While we all go as far as we can to protect our children from our extremes of emotion, including anger and upset, it would be wrong to suggest that it is healthy for individuals to keep their feelings bottled up. Clinical practice suggests that the suppression of very powerful emotions can lead to significant lowering of mood, which can, at the extreme, slip into clinical depression.

What I would suggest is that, as far as possible, these feelings are kept under control when dealing with the children but, at the earliest opportunity individuals are sought out with whom it is safe to ventilate these negative and powerful feelings. In this situation, family and friends can be important release valves for dispersing anger and upset, without themselves becoming overwhelmed in the process. I am not suggesting that simply ventilating these feelings will make everything okay, but that if these feelings are stored up in the short term for the sake of the children they still need to be acknowledged and expressed. Short-term control is also, of course, highly desirable in other areas of our lives, such as in the workplace.

As the individual comes to terms with the new situation in which they find themselves, these intense emotional reactions can be a spur for the individual to move on in their lives and away from a relationship that may once have been pleasurable but, because it has been taken from them, has now degenerated into a source of distress. If an individual remains stuck in this angry phase for too long then, instead of being an emotion that can be used productively, it can become very damaging for the individual and leaves them unable to move on from a place that is unproductive for themselves, for their children and, indeed, for anyone else around them.

I am finding it hard to say anything positive about my ex. What should I say to the children about him?

As we have noted throughout this book, it can be very difficult to retain positive feelings about someone who has left, possibly under very difficult circumstances. That ex-partner may have rapidly replaced you with someone else in their life or, indeed, that someone else may have been a contributory factor in that partner leaving. We have also looked at the emotional, social and economic impacts of that partner leaving, which are rarely positive factors.

It should be understood that there is little to be gained from allowing our own negativity to be transmitted to the children – it does nothing to help our own emotional self and it burdens the children with issues that they are not equipped to deal with. Therefore, as far as possible, parents should look at the children and the relationship they have with an absent, but nevertheless 'forever', parent, and seek to support that ongoing relationship.

Obviously, positive comments are most constructive, followed by neutral comments, with negative comments being very unhelpful indeed. It may well be that the best we can achieve is being able to make neutral comments about the ex-partner to the child.

However, we are only human and, on occasions, it may be impossible not to make negative comments about the ex-partner. What I would suggest is that you try to keep these comments to the minimum and at some later stage, as soon as you are under control again, the children may need a cuddle and to be told: 'Yes, I am angry with mum, but that is okay. I still hope that you like her and I will do what I can to make sure that you keep the relationship going with her.'

The occasional ventilation of negative emotions may not be as damaging as one would think. However, persistent negative comments about an ex-partner will have an undesirable impact on the children and could be to the detriment of the relationship between them.

I am sure my ex is slagging me off to the children. It feels awful. What can I do about it?

Following on from the above one can see that one's ex might be saying negative things to the children for at least two very different reasons.

One is that the ex is so upset and angry about the breakdown that they are simply, at times, unable to contain their feelings about you and this spills out on to the children. Hopefully, this will be short lived, and following a particular outburst, one's ex partner was able to cuddle the children and say: 'I'm sorry. I am angry at mum (or dad) but really I shouldn't have given it all to you to worry about.' In those sorts of instances, little damage is done.

As has been emphasised throughout this book, it is hoped that both parents treat the management of children following marital breakdown or relationship breakdown as seriously as they do their own separation. However, people sometimes make very elaborate plans for the ending of their relationship and moving on elsewhere but the children's needs get lost and are simply not planned for or thought about. Therefore, the obvious solution to the problem is to either establish, or maintain, communication with the ex-partner so that you can share your thoughts on the impact that the separation is having on the children.

However, it can be the case that, for whatever reason, an ex-partner is deliberately saying negative things about you to the children and this is a very different sort of problem. If the ex-partner is undermining you in front of the children and is not prepared to talk to you, then the ex-partner still needs to be made aware – face to face, by letter or by some other means – that how they are behaving is damaging the children. Hopefully this will be enough to bring the ex-partner to their senses and make them refrain from such silly behaviour.

If these are not effective strategies, as the last resort one may have to turn to the legal arena to solve this problem (see Chapter 9 on Family Mediation).

I feel so depressed about the split that I'm finding it difficult to cope. What should I do?

Most people feel low following the breakdown of this significant relationship; it is understandable and perfectly normal.

Sharing your distress with family and friends can help. They will help you to recognise that life will go on and that there will be happiness for you beyond the relationship. Coming to terms with this can be slow but it is, nevertheless, possible. Achieving in other areas of one's life – such as getting a job, or continuing to work if one is already working, as well as engaging in other outside work and home pursuits – can be very rewarding and help the individual to understand that they are a competent, whole person. The fact that their partner has left does not mean they are less valuable or valued than when they were in the relationship.

Feeling angry, sad, upset or whatever does not, of itself, require professional intervention. Having said that, for some individuals low mood can slip into a clinical depression. I would suggest that in those circumstances the general practitioner, who will be very familiar with the management of marital breakdown, should be turned to as the primary source of help. GPs can be very supportive individuals within their own right and, of course, they are also able to prescribe, if they feel it appropriate, antidepressant medication to help the patient through the worst. As well as this, GPs often have access to counsellors within the practice who may be able to provide therapeutic intervention aimed at helping the individual through this difficult phase.

However, it is worth repeating that having to resort to medication and/or counselling is only necessary in a very small number of cases and for most people the negative moods they experience following breakdown will lessen of their own accord as the individual begins to pick up on life again.

I can't stand that thought that my children will be meeting my ex's new girlfriend. How do I cope with these feelings?

One can well understand why very negative feelings would be in the air in these circumstances, especially if that new boyfriend or girlfriend was somehow involved in the marital breakdown. However, it must be recognised early on that it is almost inevitable that the children will be expected to meet with your ex-partner's new girlfriend/boyfriend, just you would want them to meet any new partner that you have.

You must take a very calm and careful look at yourself to understand where the anger and upset is coming from. You must then consider the situation and ask yourself if it would be fair to let the children know how desperately unhappy you are about them seeing your ex's new partner. Often, on reflection, parents come to the conclusion that it is indeed unreasonable to inflict their feelings on the children and are then able to send their children off with the hope that they come back having enjoyed time with their mum/dad and new partner.

However, we cannot expect people to be superhuman, and the negative feelings surrounding this issue need to be expressed, probably very forcefully, but to others rather than the children. This again is where family and friends can be excellent sources of support. It may well be the case that, when the children have gone off to dad or mum and the new partner, you take yourself off with a friend or colleague to enjoy a liberating session of slagging off the ex-partner, the new boyfriend/girlfriend or just the world in general.

Another coping mechanism would be simply to use the opportunity to go off and do something fun that takes your mind off the issue at hand. This is far more productive and provides a better framework for you to gain control of your emotions and move on in life.

How can I introduce my new partner to the children in a sensitive way?

As noted in earlier sections, it is advisable to forewarn your ex-partner that the children are to be introduced to your new partner. It is difficult to conceive of a worse way to find out that your children have met a new partner than by having it announced by the children when you next see them.

Therefore, opening a dialogue, or maintaining a dialogue, with your ex-partner is the way to go about this. He or she will need to be told who the children are going to meet and the circumstances in which they will meet. You should ask your ex-partner if he or she would find it possible to give the children permission for this meeting, explaining that this would clearly be to the children's benefit.

However, we have to be realistic and recognise that it may well be the case that the children are introduced to a new partner against the background of their other parent not being at all happy about it. What I would suggest is that during initial stages, contact is kept to a minimum and done on an activity basis where the partner joins in with something that you and the children are involved with.

Children need time to adjust to new partners and it may well be the case that the children dictate the speed at which the relationship develops. If things go favourably, all well and good, but you must be prepared for a backlash in that if your ex-partner is giving the children a hard time when they return home, particularly if they are enjoying meeting your new partner, then for a while it might be the case that the children should not meet your new partner. Once matters have calmed, emotions have been dealt with, and all the individuals involved are able to take on board the reality of this new relationship, contact can be reintroduced.

If it seems that your ex-partner will never be happy about contact between the children and your partner, then you will have to assess what the children can cope with in terms of not only meeting with a new partner, but also dealing with repercussions if they are put under pressure when they are back with your ex.

Your new partner must be aware when you embark on a relationship that you do not come as an individual and take this fully into account. You might be a single person in the sense of no longer being in a marital or long-term relationship, but they must understand that you come complete with children and any relationship they have with you has to accommodate these children that you will have forever.

My family has not been supportive over the split and now I feel very isolated. What should I do about this?

We are all well aware that over the last few decades divorce has not only become more common, but is also more socially acceptable. However, in our parents' or grandparents' generation, divorce was rare, difficult and actively frowned upon. Many people took the view that marriage was entered into for life. This was fine for those whose marriages were happy and successful, but for others who were not so lucky it was nearly always a case of 'You've made your bed, now lie in it'. Nowadays this attitude prevails much less and individuals are more likely to leave relationships that are not meeting their needs.

Even now, some parents and grandparents can find the breakdown of a relationship and divorce far too difficult to cope with and they absent themselves from their separating children or grandchildren. Clearly this can be very hurtful indeed and, for many people, more painful than the divorce itself and the loss of a partner.

It is very difficult to tackle this issue directly, other than to appeal to your parents and grandparents and try to explain why you have done what you have done, or why your partner left you. If your parents and grandparents can accept this, and continue to support you, all well and good, but if not then it is unlikely that there is any further action you can take to bring about any change. However, feelings on the matter may settle with the passage of time, and your parents or grandparents may come to you for reconciliation and to continue some sort of relationship.

It should, of course, be recognised that for some wider family members the breakdown of your relationship will be a personal loss for them, too, though it is unlikely to be as significant. They may have become very fond of your ex-partner over the years and are now saddened by the knowledge that he or she will in all probability no longer be a part of their lives. In addition, the breakdown may have come as a complete surprise to them (couples frequently conceal the state of their marriage from those outside the immediate family) and they are likely to be confronting this unwelcome news after you have had a chance to accept the breakdown and absorb at least some of the distress it has caused. This does not really excuse their withdrawal at a time when you are probably in great need of support but it may make it a little more understandable.

In some cases the breakdown of relationships is irreversible and certain family members are lost forever. There is little individuals can do about this, other to than try and create a life without that family member and let it be known that you are available should they wish to re-establish relationships. Here, again, other family and friends can help to fill the void, although a person can never be wholly replaced by another.

There is little point in beating yourself up over this. Individuals have their own difficulties and responses to situations and you are not responsible for the behaviour of your own mother, father or grandparents.

Why should I have to cope with the kids?

Although parents may continue to love their children dearly, following family breakdown and finding themselves in a one-parent family, they may also feel very resentful indeed about having to provide the full-time care for the children while the other parent appears to be swanning off and having a single life.

I think the resentment is perfectly understandable, particularly when it is associated with issues such as the parent recognising that now they have to be both mum and dad to the children and provide single-handedly all the restrictions and controls as well as the love and the care that the children need.

This is intimately linked with the next question.

It's okay for him! Why should he only see them for a few hours of fun?

This sort of question is often raised by parents and reflects the issue that the parent who is caring for the children full time often has to provide the controls and discipline that the children need, while the children go off for a few hours a week to have contact with the absent parent who simply sees that as a time of fun. It is also highly likely that the absent parent, not wanting to cause any disruption during this time, does not lay down particular boundaries; then the children return, possibly in very high spirits, to the remaining parent who is now the position of having to bring them back to ordinary life by reintroducing the word 'no'.

It is very unfair on the parent who has their day-to-day care that the children often paint him or her as the villain of the piece because when they go off to the absent parent it is all fun and laughter.

The parent seeing the child at contact must do everything they can to support the remaining parent, and in particular to maintain and reinforce boundaries put in place by that parent. There is also no reason why the parent who no longer lives full time with the children shouldn't continue to participate in the less pleasurable aspects of family life such as helping with homework, accompanying children to the dentist or hairdresser, and ferrying to activities. It will also do the children no harm if contact times are not always wall-to-wall fun but they are included in those essential but slightly boring domestic activities such as going to the supermarket and doing the laundry.

It should be acknowledged that these days children often have a very full school day and, especially if they are also participating in after-school activities such as sports clubs, Brownies and Cubs, or music or dancing lessons, they are likely to be quiet tired at weekends and need to spend at least part of the time resting and recovering. It is therefore not in the best interests of the child to cram too much activity and excitement into contact periods.

It could be the case that a parent has concerns about how the other parent is caring for the child. While these concerns should always be addressed, they must be raised with the other parent, not with the child. A child could easily perceive being cross-examined by one parent about the care he or she receives while with the other as an attempt to undermine that parent and make the child take sides. This does not help anyone.

My kids are angry at me because we have had to sell our house after the divorce. What can I tell them?

The short answer is that we have to tell them the truth. However, the way in which we do that will, of course, depend on the age and developmental stage of the child.

For all children, a simple statement needs to be made that, because of the break-up in the relationship and mummy and daddy having to live in separate houses, there is simply not the money available to keep the house that they have lived in. One would then go on to explain to the children that, although they have to move to a new house, they will still be able to live together and to maintain the loving relationships that already exist.

As far as possible, effort will have been made to move to a house in the same locality so the children can continue in their present schools. Of course, if the new house is in a totally different area, the children will not only lose the parent who has left, but also their home, their schoolmates and, of course, the school itself. One can well understand why children would be extremely angry under these circumstances and, as we have said throughout, it is important that all concerned have the opportunity to ventilate these very powerful emotions, as suppressing them can have a significant negative effect on the individual experiencing these emotions.

Therefore, we can take a different view of the children's expressions of 'anger' and look upon it as perfectly reasonable and appropriate, and absorb their anger as best one can while recognising that though it may be voiced to you, particularly if you are the one available, it is not necessarily meant for you. While this may be unpleasant, it can nevertheless be seen as a necessary state of affairs and at least allows the children to ventilate their anger to someone who is better able to cope with it than they are.

Of course, this may be occurring at a time when you're feeling angry, your mood is low, and you feel less equipped than you have ever been in your life to manage anyone else's emotions. It can be very helpful to marshal the resources of family and friends to support you as an individual going through this difficult time, and maybe to support the children too and become involved in explaining to them why things are the way they are. I am not suggesting that of itself this will make the children feel better but at least they can gain a level of understanding that it is not necessarily your fault, or your entire fault, but you are nevertheless able, along with others, to help them with their negative feelings.

I am sure attempts will have been made to put as positive a spin on a change of home as was possible to help the children understand that a move to a new house, new school and new area and finding new friends can be exciting, not necessarily the awful scenario they are imagining.

All this is hard but necessary work that will help children through this difficult phase. If all else fails, when your child shrieks at you, take comfort in the fact that this is healthier than if they were sitting in a corner too miserable to express how they feel. I would far prefer to deal with an overtly angry child than a very sad or depressed child.

I want my children to have contact with my ex-husband but he doesn't seem interested. What can I do?

There can be several reasons why your ex-husband, or ex-wife, does not want to have ongoing contact with the children.

Thankfully this is not that common, but for some individuals it can simply be the case that having contact, but in a limited way, is just too painful. They therefore block any overtures concerning contact and attempt to withdraw entirely from their children. Obviously, the solution is to help the parent concerned recognise that, as an ongoing loving parent, they have to submit to these less than ideal conditions to help the children maintain a positive view of their father and to ensure their children's future well-being. The parent may well need reminding that both adults are expecting the children to come to terms with all the new arrangements and striving to ensure them that they will in time come to accept and tolerate them, and the same can equally apply to a distressed adult.

These are easy words that can be difficult to put into practice and it may be the case that the ex-partner is not the one who is best placed to convey these messages. Family and friends should be asked to rally round to support the ex-partner and encourage an ongoing relationship with the children.

However, we must also face head on the reality that some individuals are not nice people. There are those who are quite prepared to abandon their children if it is the price that has to be paid for embarking on a new life. There is no excusing this, and no good psychological reasons that can be put forward to explain their behaviour other than the fact that they have simply finished with that relationship and they have moved on. Nothing is going to induce that individual to re-engage in a relationship with their children.

In terms of what one does about a relationship than cannot be preserved, then it needs to be explained to the children that the ex-partner is not able to maintain the relationship, as in the first scenario, or does not want to, as in the second scenario. Obviously, how this is conveyed depends on the age of the child but, nevertheless the child at some stage has to be presented with the truth and allowed to come to terms with it. I recognise that there can be a backlash for the parent still caring for the child but this falls into the areas already discussed of how we deal with our children's expressions of anger and upset.

My children are having contact with their father but my new partner is unsupportive of it. How should I deal with it?

It should have been made clear at the outset of your new relationship that you have children and an ex-partner and that the children have an ongoing relationship with you and their other parent. Hopefully your new partner will have accepted this and taken you on as a package and not entirely as an individual.

But if this isn't the way it's working out, it may well be the case that the new partner initially felt he could move into a new family and cope with the prevailing circumstances but subsequently found he was aggrieved with the ex-partner for some reason, such as lack of emotional or financial support or the circumstances in which the partner left you. Here we can see that, though the new partner is being supportive of you and may even be expressing well-founded anger and upset, it is not being done in an appropriate way. If they do have strong feelings they should voice them in terms of upset at how the ex-partner has behaved or is behaving, rather than interfering in contact between the children and their parent.

A new partner needs to recognise what he is doing and why, and if it is genuinely the case that he is upset on behalf of the new partner, then so be it. However, new partners who move into a family and then feel that they can dictate relationships within the family are probably not good partners.

My kids keep asking me why my ex and I can't get back together. How do I cope with this?

Even parents who separated following an acrimonious period at home will often find their children saying that they would prefer it if mum and dad got back together again.

If the parents have maintained a dialogue with each other following the separation then hopefully they would both be able to convey to the children that, sadly, mummy and daddy don't love each other any more and won't be getting back together again, but that they both love the children a great deal and that won't change. Even young children have some understanding of what it is like to fall out with people and to find friendships coming to an end. Whereas, obviously, this does not carry the entire essence of the end of a marital relationship, children can nevertheless see no longer being friends with someone doesn't mean that everyone else has to dislike that friend too.

If, however, the other partner cannot, or does not want to, be involved in this dialogue then, sadly, you are going to have to deal with this in the same way but on your own.

My children want my ex-husband to visit for Christmas but I can't bear the thought. What should I do?

If it is possible to have the ex-partner in the family home then, of course, this can be a pleasant time for the children, provided they understand that the marriage is still over and this is not mummy and daddy getting back together again.

However, unless you are absolutely certain that it would be a success, think very hard about this. Many very unpleasant scenarios have been created when ex-partners have returned for an occasion such as Christmas and, within a very short time, pent-up anger and emotions have come to the fore and children have witnessed unpleasant situations culminating with the ex-partner storming out or being thrown out.

If you think there is the slightest possibility of this happening, then it is better not to allow it in the first place. The children must be made to understand that, though it's perfectly fine to go off and spend time with mum or dad and then come home again, even if this takes place on Christmas Day, having mummy and daddy in the same place on Christmas Day is not a good idea and is not going to happen. You don't have to provide all the details of your reasons, but the message does need to be clear and unambiguous.

The children feel very angry with their father as he was the one who left us. What should I do about these feelings?

What you can do about these feelings depends upon whether you have maintained an ongoing dialogue with your ex-partner or not.

If you have maintained a dialogue then you need to talk about how you are both going to discuss this with the children. The children need to be told calmly and accurately about enough of the facts of the breakdown to allow them to begin to express their feelings about the parent that left, and indeed about the remaining parent.

If there is no ongoing communication between you, then it may be left to you alone to discuss with the children why dad left and the circumstances under which he left. This will help the children to maintain a more reasonable understanding of the situation and will hopefully allay this biased anger that they are feeling.

Another possibility is that you have maintained a dialogue with your ex-partner, but he totally denies any responsibility for the breakdown of the relationship. In this case you are faced with the more complex problem of having to explain to the children why it is the marriage came to an end, but in the knowledge that this may be rejected or refuted by your ex-partner.

We should understand that it may well be the case that you are the person they can be angry at, simply because dad isn't there at the right time or because it is safer to be angry with you. When children go off to contact, it can resemble a mini holiday during which they may not be checked but are allowed free rein, possibly because the parent they are visiting doesn't want to do anything that may prevent the children wanting to come back again. By the same token, children may not want to be overtly angry at that parent because, if they are, then the parent may not want to continue with contact.

My ex wants contact with the children but they are saying they don't want to go. Do I have to force them?

The short answer to this is yes, given that it is better for the children to have an ongoing relationship with an absent parent than not. However, the more realistic answer is that we need to understand why the children are saying they don't want to go to contact.

The children may have many and varied reasons: they would rather stay at home with you; they feel upset and angry with your ex-partner; they don't like where there mum or dad has gone to live; they don't like dad's new partner or her children; they don't want to do the boring things that they may be expected to do with dad; they wanted to do something with their friends in the area in which they live. The children need to be asked, though not cross-examined, as to why they are being a bit resistant about going to contact so that action can be taken to overcome the difficulties identified.

If the child says that they prefer to stay at home, it could be that he or she is worried about you and needs to be reassured that you will be fine even though you will be pleased to see them when they return. If going to contact means that they will be missing out on activities in their home location then perhaps it is time for the details of the contact days and times to be adjusted. This could particularly be the case where older children are concerned.

The issue of children having difficulties with an absent parent's new partner and/or that partner's children has been dealt with in Chapter 6 on New Families. The situation needs to be reviewed, and the solution may be for the children to go off to see their mum and dad without the new partner, who arranges to be doing something else during contact time.

If the children are simply bored during contact, then the ex-partner can be helped to plan more interesting activities that would make the children happier and more likely to go to contact.

A more difficult slant on this problem is whether you are giving messages to the children that you do not wish them to go to contact. This will be easy to recognise if you have, deliberately or otherwise, put obstacles in the way of contact by word or deed. For example, you might have made disparaging comments about your ex-partner, or said to the children that you'd rather they stayed with you, or, more subtly, you may have generated more interesting alternatives to keep the children at home. This may take the form of: 'If you weren't going to dad's we could have done this, that or the other.'

Clearly, even unwittingly giving messages about your negative feelings concerning contact is not in the children's best interest. You must take a good and honest look inside yourself and question if this is what you are doing. This isn't easy and you may need to talk it through with family and friends.

Of course, if you realise that you are discouraging contact on purpose, this must stop forthwith and the children need to be given permission to go off to mum or dad's.

Having established that there is really no good reason why the children shouldn't go to contact, even if they are a little unwilling, there is still the question of how to make them go. I often hear extremely competent parents saying 'I find it impossible to get the children to contact with their dad'. However, when I ask them what they would do if their children woke up tomorrow and said they didn't want to go to school, they often reply: 'They've got to go to school, so of course they'll go.' Similarly if the parent is asked what they would do if a child had a dental appointment and said they didn't want to go, they say: 'Well, of course they have to go to the dentist. It's just something they have to do.' If you can get your children to school on a regular basis and you can get them to the dentist, the chances are you can get them to contact.

The qualification to this is, of course, if something unpleasant is happening in contact, which would need to be addressed (see pages 132–3).

I can't seem to talk to my ex-partner without it turning into an argument. What should I do about this?

If you are finding it impossible to communicate civilly, then you may have to resort to mediation services or even move into the legal arena (see Chapters 9 and 10). However, this is a matter between the two of you and is definitely not an issue for the children. Life is tough enough for you adults and we don't need to make it tougher on the children.

Obviously you shouldn't discuss issues that may end in argument when your children are around to witness it. If your ex-partner is returning them home, bite your tongue, be civil, be as pleasant as possible, and leave what you need to say for another time.

My children saw my ex-partner hit me the other day. What effect is this likely to have on them?

Being attacked by anyone is unacceptable. Being attacked by an ex-partner in front of one's children is even more deplorable.

Surprisingly, the severity of an attack is not a good indicator of how severely children will react to it. Some children will, superficially at least, seem to be very little affected by seeing a serious assault, whereas others find 'mild' acts of violence very distressing and disturbing indeed.

Witnessing a violent act is an extremely traumatic experience for children and can lead to emotional difficulties such as becoming distrusting of others, developing sleep disturbances, bedwetting, and just generally becoming upset, unhappy and distressed. There can be other significant, but more subtle, effects such as the children losing respect for you, having watched how you have been treated disrespectfully, in this case by their father. Some children can identify very strongly with the abuser and, in this case, take on the role of the abuser and become verbally and/or physically violent towards you too. One can, therefore, well understand why individuals would seek to stop a child going to contact visits with an ex-partner who has demonstrated that degree of violence.

As discussed earlier, if children are reluctant to go to contact, we need to establish why. If it is because they are frightened of someone whom they have seen is capable of violence, that, of itself, may be a perfectly reasonable and legitimate reason for the children not to go to contact.

Of course, issues of violence and abuse should never be taken lightly and need very careful assessment. This is when the Court may well become involved and an officer of the Children and Family Court Advisory and Support Service (CAFCASS) asked to meet with family members to prepare a report for the Court, or reports may be commissioned from psychiatrists, psychologists or other specialists to determine the level of risk assessment the husband (in this case) presents to either the parent or the children.

The direct and indirect effect on children of violence needs to be understood in its fullest context. One of the indirect effects is that if a mother is living in constant fear of a violent ex-partner, it may significantly impair her capacity to care for her children and, as such, may require the issue of contact to be very carefully thought about, and whether the contact is meeting the children's needs. If the impact on the mother is of significant severity then a decision would have to be made as to whether ongoing contact with the father is in the children's overall interest.

I am stuck in an unhappy relationship but some people think I should stick it out for the sake of the children. How can I know what's best?

No one else can tell you whether or not you should stay in a relationship. You have to come to that decision yourself.

If you feel that you can continue in that relationship, do it for you, not for the children. Children should never be used as a reason to stay in or get out of a relationship. That has to be your responsibility and your responsibility alone. Having said that, I would add that if you decide to stay in the relationship you must ensure it works to meet the needs of the children. Similarly, if you leave the relationship, then the likely repercussions on the children need to be carefully thought through by you and your partner so they can be minimised.

What I would suggest is that you consider whether it is worth staying in a relationship 'for the sake of the children' if they are going to be living with a miserable mum and dad who will be bickering and niggling at each other or, at worst, becoming overtly angry and upset with each other, which may result in violence. Compare this with the children living separate from one parent, hopefully with ongoing contact, where the parent with whom they are living is more relaxed and calm and more in control of their life.

Some will say this is simplistic and fails to recognise the social and economic implications of separation. However, my overriding interest is in the overall well-being of the children. Of course, like everyone else, in the ideal world I would hope that mum and dad would be happy together and be a well-functioning unit in which they can care for their children adequately. But I am well aware that well-functioning one-parent families are also very good at bringing up children: two-parent families where there is significant disharmony are not good at bringing up children.

My children refuse to talk to me about the break-up. What should I do about it?

The first question to ask here is, are the children functioning as well as one would reasonably expect? If the answer is yes, then perhaps there is nothing to worry about and there is no need to pursue this. It is always possible that the children are bored silly with the whole break-up and are not talking about it simply because they want to move on with their little lives. However, if a child who refuses to talk about the break-up does not appear to be coping well, then this needs sensitive and careful handling.

We have recognised throughout this book that emotional upset when a marriage comes to an end is not only expected but is perfectly normal for all concerned. We have also sought to emphasise the importance of finding a safe means to express these emotions because suppressed emotions can be driven inwards, leading to the lowering of mood. This is as true for children as it is for adults.

If you believe that your child is struggling and suffering significantly, you need to think carefully about the way forward. One would hope that attempts are made to discuss this with the child but, obviously since this is the major factor in this case, the child may not be co-operative.

We often think that parents are the ones that children should confide in, but actually it is surprising how much easier they can find it to convey what they are feeling to family and friends. Therefore, I would suggest that route is tried first. If that fails, consideration should then be given to approaching the child's general practitioner with a view to gaining access to more specialist resources to help the child, through verbal or non-verbal therapeutic work, to express what he or she is experiencing. However, the proportion of children who require this kind of service is very small indeed and most survive perfectly well with good support from their wider family and friends.

Many children go through a quiet phase following the break-up of their parents' marriage. Like their parents, children are a bit more resilient than we sometimes think and they nearly always work through the process with the ongoing love and support of both parents, even if they are not living together, or with the ongoing love and support of one parent if the other one fails to engage.

My daughter has started wetting the bed recently. Is this because of the break-up?

It could be. We recognise that children can be very upset and distressed when their parents split and separate. How different children express this emotion will vary, just as it does amongst adults. Bedwetting in children is an indicator of ongoing emotional upset. If you feel this might be the cause, it may be helpful to explore with the child the nature of their upset and help them find ways of expressing this with a parent or other family, friends or school contacts.

However, I would raise a word of caution and recognise that, although marital breakdown can be very upsetting, not every problem may stem from it. Other areas of the child's life need to be explored in terms of ongoing relationships at school or with friends and one should never ignore physical issues; it may be the case that a visit to the GP would establish that the child has a urinary tract infection.

If the child is eventually able to verbalise how they are feeling and recognise how are upset they are, then clearly this can be most easily dealt with with the usual kisses and cuddles and ongoing support from a parents or parents.

One of the teachers said my son was crying at school but he wouldn't say what was wrong. What can I do about this?

Upset at school could be related to the marital breakdown. However, we should avoid automatically assuming that every problem is related to the separation and explore the usual issues – at school, at home and elsewhere – that occur in any child's life. It is heartbreaking to think of your child being so miserable he cries but doesn't speak, whatever the cause is, and he needs help to express whatever it is he is feeling in a more constructive manner.

I just feel generally down and I have no energy. How can I motivate myself to be cheerful around the children?

First you need to establish whether the lethargy and sadness you are feeling are within the normal range, or whether you may be slipping into clinical depression. It may be difficult for you to evaluate this for yourself, so I would suggest an appointment with your GP, who will be able to make some sort of assessment.

If it is the case that you are simply sad and unhappy and generally despondent, my first reaction would be: 'Well, why on earth do you need to be permanently cheerful around the children?' During the break-up phase anyone would expect you to be feeling pretty low and awful. The issue here is simply being able to share with all concerned, including the children, that you are feeling a bit down and tired and could they bear with you for a while until you get back to your normal self again. Don't beat yourself up because you are not the person you thought you were before the break-up. Before long you will be that person again, the cheerful individual who has the energy to do the things you want to do, and in the meantime don't make yourself feel even worse by adding on guilt that, in some way, you are failing your children.

If you love your children, if you give them sufficient cuddles and explain to them that it is nothing they have done, and you will be okay in a while, I don't think you need do any more than that.

If, however, what you are feeling goes beyond what is normal in the circumstances, your GP is there to support you by providing support, medication or onward referral to specialist services.

I am sure that a split between my husband and me is imminent. Should I talk to the children about this?

This is an interesting question and my first thought was, should the question really be should *we* talk to the children about this. It is rarely the case that the deterioration of a relationship comes as a surprise to the partners. Both will have been living in the midst of unpleasantness, unhappiness and general distress. There may have been angry outbursts or sullen silences or perhaps a mixture of both.

As has been emphasised throughout this book, parents are parents forever and, even in the midst of deep trauma in terms of the deterioration in their relationship, the children need to be to the fore. However, as we discussed in terms of preparing for the breakdown of the marriage, at some point you will have to stop trying to protect the children from all knowledge that things are not as they should be and they will need to be informed, at some level, why things are happening within the family the way they are.

When children are told that that change is likely to happen, though the exact nature of the change may be still be unknown, they need to be reassured that both their mum and dad will continue to love them, even though mum and dad are finding it very difficult, if not impossible, to care for each other. Both parents need to be involved in this; if one parent is left making all the reassuring noises, then the parent who has opted out should recognise that he or she is not doing the best by their children.

My daughter asked me the other day if her daddy and I were going to split up. How should I answer her?

The must be answered as honestly as is possible and appropriate to the child's level of understanding.

For example, if mum and dad are going through a bad time but are trying to make it work, trying to patch things up and move on to a better relationship, then it may be appropriate to tell the children just that, provided it is in language they can understand. Tell them that hopefully things will end up okay between you and your partner but whatever happens the children will always be loved and cared for.

If matters have gone beyond trying to resolve and the split is imminent, then children need to be forewarned as indicated above. Lots and lots of reality-based reassurance needs to be given.

My children are behaving really badly since the split. Will this stop?

The short answer to this is yes, probably – providing they are given the structure, the boundaries and the reassurance that they need.

We have recognised throughout this book that it is only to be expected that individuals, including the children, are upset and distressed at the breakdown of a marriage and the moving out of one parent. Exactly how the children deal with this may be highly variable but one can predict that they will go through a difficult phase and come out the other end.

Of course, if they receive ongoing support from both parents, they are likely to recover more easily and more quickly than if they are supported by only one parent, especially if that parent is struggling on their own. As we identified earlier, however well the parent or parents are coping, using family and friends and the school to support the family is a perfectly good and responsible way of managing.

In terms of the words 'behaving really badly', I would suggest that we need to understand what the children are doing and recognise that they may not be being deliberately difficult, wilful or badly behaved. What we are seeing may be a demonstration of the degree of upset that they are experiencing. Reinterpreting it as distressed behaviour rather than bad behaviour may make it easier to understand and deal with.

Nevertheless, all children need boundaries and, while we bend over backwards to ensure that they feel understood, loved and cared for, nevertheless there are limits and once the children reach or transcend those boundaries they have to be brought back under control. If we do not do this, the children will simply be indulged and they will feel even less secure than they did when the parents were taking the trouble to set limits. While children may not welcome boundaries, they do respond to them and appear to feel safer and more contained than when they are left to their own devices.

Intervening when a child is behaving in a distressed or difficult manner will let them know that, while you understand and have a degree of compassion, that child is approaching or has reached or even exceeded the acceptable limit.

Why should I let my kids see my ex when he's not paying me any maintenance?

Most parents can readily see that maintenance has little to do with ongoing relationships between parent and child, but I regularly hear this assertion made more often out of sheer frustration than wilfulness. I have known of excellent and very competent parents attempting to stop contact over issues of maintenance, though they soon realise that this was the wrong thing to do. Their frustration shines through when they say such things as 'It's the only weapon I've got'.

I can well understand the thinking behind the statement but, in fairness to the children, they should not be used as a weapon in a financial, or any other, dispute. These disputes are 'grown-up stuff' and should not involve the children. I recognise that this is stating the obvious, but these things do sometimes need to be said, particularly at times when parents are functioning less well than they would be normally.

Why should I send my kids to see my ex when he is being abusive to them?

A section of this book is devoted to the issues involving the legal process and those thankfully rare circumstances when there are issues beyond the norm that need to be considered (see pages 132–3 and 139–40).

The use of the word 'abuse' is serious and is often a blanket term for emotional abuse, neglect, sexual abuse or physical abuse. If a parent legitimately thought that their child was at risk of abuse, in whatever form, from the other parent, then it is almost certain that the Court would want to investigate matters fully and may instruct an officer of the Children and Family Court Advisory and Support Service (CAFCASS) or the social services to carry out an independent assessment of the situation.

It is likely that ongoing contact arrangements will be heavily influenced by those assessment reports and judgements made as to what is in the best interest of the child, including whether contact should take place or not.

Part Two

The Legal Aspects

This section looks at some of the problems of divorce from the legal standpoint, focusing on problems that can occur when things do not go quite as smoothly as anyone would hope. Most families will not have to cope with these issues, but this advice will be useful for those who have been less fortunate.

CHAPTER 8

When Does the Law
Become Involved?

Happily, most divorces in Britain proceed with only a minimal input from the legal services. A divorce is only possible once a decree absolute has been ordered by a Court, but on a practical level this very rarely requires the parties themselves to attend at Court. Most divorces are straightforward and can be dealt with by solicitors, who will fill in the necessary paperwork on your behalf. The only time it becomes necessary for divorcing couples to attend at Court is if there is disagreement over finances or the children (or occasionally the granting of the divorce itself) that cannot be resolved through negotiation.

The last thing that either of the authors of this book wishes to do is to encourage families to run to the Courts to resolve their differences. Family law is not about creating conflict, it is about reaching workable and lasting arrangements wherever this is possible. It is a truism that any arrangement that has been reached through amicable discussion and mutual compromise is far more likely to be successful than any decision that has been imposed by the Courts. It is hoped that many of you will be able to use the information contained within this book as a tool to help you discuss the arrangements for the children, and come to an agreement without the need for any outside intervention.

However, if that were always possible, neither of the authors would be very busy in our current jobs! The reality is that the break-up of a relationship is often painful and difficult and can lead to feelings of anger, depression or resentment. While these feelings almost invariably fade with time, it can be very difficult to discuss matters rationally with an ex whom you feel is being unreasonable or who has treated you unfairly. If that is the case, or for any other reason you feel that an agreement about the children's future simply won't be possible, it may be that you need the help of the mediation service or the Courts to help you reach a decision. The information that follows will help you better understand both the options that are open to you and the way the mediation and Court processes work, should you find yourself in a situation where you need to use them.

The distinctions between divorce and separation

The title of this book refers to helping your children survive your divorce, but almost all of the information contained within it will apply equally to those couples who have never been married but are separating after a long relationship. In both cases, of course, the same considerations will apply in relation to supporting your children through the process, i.e. how best to tell the children, how to support them through the changes that they experience, and how to help them maintain a relationship with whichever parent is no longer living with the children.

However, a major difference is the way in which these couples are viewed legally in England and Wales, and the steps they have to take during the process of separation. Getting divorced is a legal process (see page 22 for the grounds for a divorce) that almost always involves having legal representation at some stage; a divorce cannot occur without a decree absolute being pronounced by the Court. Divorcing couples will, of course, need to come to an arrangement about both the finances and the children. Thankfully these issues are usually resolved through negotiation, either between the husband and wife themselves or with the help of solicitors. If no agreement is reached, it may be necessary to resort to the Courts to make decisions on these issues, though I would stress that this is by no means inevitable.

On the other hand, couples who have never been married but are separating after having lived together are not required to go through any legal procedure in order to separate. These people can end the relationship simply by living apart from each other. There is no requirement for the law to become involved at any stage. However, parents will still need to come to an arrangement about future plans for any children of the relationship. Decisions will have to be made as to which parent the children will live with and how much contact they will have with the absent parent. As there is no requirement to involve lawyers on the issue of the separation itself – unlike a divorce – it is entirely up to separating couples whether or not they choose to involve lawyers on issues to do with the children. Having said that, any parent is entitled to apply to the Court for an order for either contact or residence should they find that the issue cannot be resolved by any other means. Once again, just as for couples who have been married, most unmarried parents are able to come to a workable arrangement without needing to go to Court.

Unfortunately, though, we don't live in a perfect world. Expecting every couple in the process of separation or divorce to remain friendly and civil and talk through all their future plans would be a little idealistic. In some situations it may be that couples have to resort to the law in order to resolve differences about where the children should live and how much contact they should be having. The important point to note is that, in the main, this procedure is exactly the same for divorcing couples as for those who are separating after living together. So, in that respect, almost all the information in the book, in terms of both the emotional and the legal advice, will apply to any couple with children.

The role of the lawyer

As already explained, if you are separating from a partner after a period of cohabitation, it may well be that you never need to see a lawyer at all. Separating couples do not need to involve lawyers in the process of separation as they are free to separate as and when they choose without legal intervention. Lawyers will only become involved if there is an argument over children or money that cannot be resolved between the parties.

If you are in the process of a divorce, then the strong likelihood is that you will need a lawyer at some stage. Although 'do-it-yourself' divorces are technically possible, they are still unusual and the most usual way to get divorced is for a lawyer to take care of all the paperwork on your behalf. The lawyer you choose will ask you about the situation relating to both finances and the children. In most cases these issues can be sorted out simply through negotiation with your ex's lawyer. Decisions about the children's future will be referred to the Court only as a last resort but, for those who find that they do have to turn to the Courts, the whole procedure relating to both residence and contact issues is explained in Chapter 10.

Finding the right solicitor

The best way to find a good solicitor is always by personal recommendation. If you know anyone who has got divorced, then ask if they were happy with the service they received. Was the solicitor friendly? Did they give good advice? Were they prompt in dealing with inquiries? Did they keep their client fully informed as to what was going on?

Almost all solicitors nowadays offer a free half-hour consultation at the beginning of any case, so if you unsure as to where to start looking, this is a good opportunity to see if the solicitor is someone you think you could confide in and work with. It is particularly important in family law to find a solicitor you are comfortable with, as you may well have to discuss sensitive and personal issues in a relatively short space of time.

Some tips you might wish to bear in mind:

- Find someone with an expertise in family law. You can ask about this by ringing the firm direct, or you could look in the *Yellow Pages* for a firm that has included the initials SFLA (Solicitors' Family Law Association) in the advertisement.

- Check also that the firm has a Legal Aid Franchise for family work. Whether or not you think you might qualify for legal aid, franchises are given only to those firms that meet a strict set of criteria, and which also go through regular checks on its procedures and practices.

The legal steps to divorce

This book is not designed to explain the steps of a divorce in their entirety, as the focus is primarily on how best to support your children through the process. Should you wish to have more detailed information on what getting divorced entails, including the financial implications, then *Control Your Divorce* (Foulsham 2003) will have the answer to most of the questions you are likely to have.

Briefly, though, the steps of the divorce process are:

1. The divorce petition is filed by the Petitioner (the person who starts off the divorce process).

2. The Notice of Proceedings is sent to the Respondent (the person who receives the petition).

3. The Respondent returns the Acknowledgement of Service to the Court.

4. The Court grants a Certificate of Entitlement to a decree.

5. The Court grants a decree nisi.

6. The Court grants a decree absolute.

The time it takes to get from step 1 to step 6 can vary hugely depending on the issues involved, but a standard divorce where matters are agreed between the parties can usually be over within about four to six months of the notice of proceedings being sent. Of course, it can take considerably longer in cases where there are protracted arguments over, for instance, financial issues.

When parents can't agree

As already mentioned, most issues in a divorce can be settled through negotiation, either directly between the husband and wife themselves or through their solicitors. If, however, you simply cannot come to an agreement with your ex about the children, and if you find yourself in a situation where even negotiation between solicitors does not lead to a workable arrangement, it is still worthwhile considering the possibility of mediation (see Chapter 9) before having to resort to the Courts.

Family Mediation

Family mediation is a service available throughout the UK that is specifically designed to help divorcing and separating couples come to decisions about what their future arrangements should be without having to fight about it in Court. It is available privately and can also be funded by the Legal Services Commission for those entitled to legal aid.

Mediation can be used to discuss financial matters, but also issues relating to the future of the children such as where they should live and how contact should be arranged. It is important to note that the mediation process is completely independent of the Courts, that it is not a counselling service, and that it does not exist to get couples back together or to offer legal advice. It is there to identify matters that are in dispute, and to help couples come to a mutually acceptable agreement about these matters wherever possible.

Mediators often have a legal background, but they have also gone through specific training in order to qualify as mediators. The skill of the mediator is to identify where the common ground lies and to help couples reach a compromise that both can live with wherever this is possible. Mediation gives both couples an equal chance to air their views and express any concerns they might have. If a mediator thinks that counselling would help any particular couple, then they may suggest this as a possibility.

How mediation works

Both you and your ex-partner will meet with a mediator in a private and neutral setting. The idea is for the mediator to help both parties raise any issues they might have in a non-confrontational way, to explain their concerns and worries and to discuss all the relevant issues with someone there to guide the discussions and attempt to prevent conflict and hostility wherever possible. A mediator will ensure that both people get the chance to put their point of view across, so that even if one of the couple has always dominated conversations or arguments before, this should not be the case during a mediation session.

When mediation is appropriate

Don't think that you have to wait until crisis point to turn to the mediation service; you can approach it at any time during the divorce or separation process. Even if you have already issued legal proceedings, do not let this put you off considering mediation. Courts are very willing to allow couples time to attempt agreement through mediation if they indicate a willingness to try. It is a fallacy to think that family Courts wish to encourage confrontation between parents; they do not, and in fact Courts encourage agreement and compromise wherever possible.

The effectiveness of mediation

Mediation is most likely to work when both parents go into it with a positive attitude, and with a view to reaching a compromise. That said, there is no guarantee that you will leave mediation with a perfect agreement. You will know your own level of commitment to the process, but you cannot control your ex's willingness to engage in mediation, and in some cases the break-up may have been so bitter that mediation simply cannot iron out your differences. If one partner is simply not prepared to countenance mediation, then it is almost certain to fail.

Another important point is that neither party should feel threatened or dominated by the other. So if, for example, you have been in a relationship that has involved domestic violence or serious emotional abuse, it may be that mediation is not appropriate.

If you have any doubts as to whether or not mediation would work in your particular case, then you should phone your local mediation service to discuss the situation (see pages 151–2). You will be able to talk through your concerns before starting the mediation process either on your own or together with your ex.

The cost

There is no standard fee for mediation. Most mediators offer a free first appointment with an hourly rate thereafter. Your local mediation service will be able to supply you with the rates applicable in your local area.

As already mentioned, you may qualify for help from the Legal Services Commission to cover mediation costs, and some services also offer bursaries that you can apply for if you are on a low income and would find the cost of mediation difficult to meet without it. One certainty, though, is that any couple able to agree matters through mediation, as opposed to fighting about them through the Court system, will save hundreds of pounds in legal fees by doing so.

Finding a mediation service

There are currently around 70 mediation services situated around the UK. A good starting point is the handbook of the UK College of Family Mediators, which will be available at your local County Court. This publication contains a list of all the members of the college and their addresses. I would especially advise you to approach a mediation service that is a member of the college to ensure that it is trained in dealing with family issues in particular. You can also ring National Family Mediation (see page 151), which should also be able to help you. If you are specifically looking for a mediation service that can provide mediation through the Legal Service Commission, then you can contact the CLS on 0845 608 1122, check on their website at www.justask.org.uk or consult the Community Legal Service Directory, which is available in local libraries.

How long does the mediation process take?

No two couples will have exactly the same issues to deal with in mediation, so it would not be realistic to predict precisely how long the process should take for a particular case. On average, however, it is suggested that most couples will need up to six sessions to sort out the matters relevant to them. Each session lasts between an hour and an hour and a half, but your local mediation service will explain how the system near you is organised once you decide to approach them.

Confidentiality

You can rest assured that whatever you discuss within your mediation sessions will remain completely confidential. No one will be able to refer to anything said during mediation to anyone else or any other organisation, including the Court. Because of this, you can discuss matters freely and without risk of prejudice should you later have to resort to the Court for a final decision. The only exception to this confidentiality rule is if an issue arises during a session that makes it apparent that someone (especially a child) is at risk of serious harm, in which case the mediator will have to inform social services of the risk.

If agreement is reached

Once agreement is reached, the mediator will help the couple draw up an agreed statement that sets out exactly what has been agreed, as well as any other issues that might still be in dispute. Each partner receives a copy of this document, and a copy is also sent to each partner's solicitor. The statements are not legally binding, but should go a considerable way to assist your solicitor in drawing up a Court order that represents what you have agreed.

If mediation fails

If you have not been able to reach any workable arrangement about the future of the children either through your solicitors or through mediation, then it may be that you will have to turn to the Courts to resolve matters. Chapter 10 deals with the Court process relating to both residence and contact issues and what you might expect should you find yourself in this position.

Residence and Contact Issues

As we have already explained, between them most parents will be able to come to some sort of workable agreement about their children's future. Sometimes, though, this simply isn't possible. Usually this is because for one or both of the parties the divorce or separation has been so painful that they find themselves unable, or unwilling, to talk sensibly about where the best interests of the children lie. The aim of this chapter is certainly not to frighten you, or to make you think that you will inevitably end up in the Courts arguing about the children. In all probability you won't. However, if you do find yourself in that situation, you will find the whole process considerably easier if you know what is involved and how decisions are likely to be made.

The sorts of issues relating to children that are most often argued about are *where* they should live, *which parent* they should live with, and *how often* the other parent should have contact with them and how to go about arranging this.

The Statement of Arrangements

In divorce cases, the person who files the original divorce petition (the Petitioner) is also asked to fill in a document called the Statement of Arrangements. This is a document that asks lots of questions about the plans that the Petitioner has for all sorts of matters that relate to the children's welfare. (It should be remembered that this particular document is used only as part of divorce proceedings, so it does not apply to cohabitees.) We won't reproduce the whole form here as it's about eight pages long, but these are some of the points it will request details on:

Home details

The address at which each child lives.

Details of the number of living rooms and bedrooms etc. at each of the above addresses.

Whether the house is rented or owned, and by whom.

Whether any rent or mortgage is being paid regularly.

The names of all other persons living with the children and their relationship to the children.

Any possible changes to these arrangements.

Education and training

The names of schools/colleges currently attended by each child.

Any special educational needs the children may have.

Any possible changes to these arrangements.

Childcare

The name of the parent who looks after the children day to day.

Whether that parent goes out to work.

Who looks after the children if and when that parent is not there.

Who looks after the children in the school holidays.

Any possible changes to these arrangements.

Maintenance

Husband's/wife's contribution towards the maintenance of the children.

Whether the payment is made under a Court order.

Whether the payment follows an assessment by the Child Support Agency.

Whether maintenance for the children has been agreed.

Contact with the Children

Whether the children ever see the husband/wife.

Any possible changes to these arrangements.

Details of proposed arrangements for contact and residence.

Health

The general health of the children.

Any special health needs.

Other Court Proceedings

Whether the children are in the care of the local authority or under the supervision of a social worker.

Whether any of the children are on the Child Protection Register.

Any past or present proceedings in any Court involving the children, for example adoption, custody/residence, access/contact, care, supervision or maintenance.

As you will see, the Court is concerned to know whether there is agreement by both parents on all the vital issues affecting the children and their upbringing. Once the Petitioner has filled in this form, a copy will be sent to the Respondent so that he can see how the Petitioner has answered these points.

When the proceedings reach the stage where the judge decides that you should have the decree nisi (this is an order of the Court stating that you are entitled to a divorce), he will then go on to see whether or not he thinks the proposed arrangements for the children are satisfactory. If he does, he will then give both parties a certificate showing this. This is an important certificate as without it your decree absolute (or final divorce) is likely to be delayed.

If the judge is not satisfied with the information on the Statement of Arrangements, then he can deal with this in several different ways; he can ask for more information from either or both of the parents, he can ask for a welfare report, or in some cases he can even ask to see the parents in Court.

Children and the Court

It is highly unusual for a child to be asked to attend Court over issues on residence and contact. Very occasionally a judge might request that a child be present to speak to the judge directly, but I must stress that this is very rare.

As we have already stated, the more desirable way of resolving any issues over the children is for both parents to be able to agree between them what the best outcome should be. However, where this simply isn't possible, it may be that these matters eventually end up being resolved by a judge in Court. While it is very unusual for the divorce itself to lead to a contested Court hearing, it is more common for ex-spouses to need Court assistance over issues to do with either money or the children.

Deciding on residence issues

In the past 'custody' was the term used to describe where the children should live. You will often hear people describing cases where a parent 'had to fight for custody'. Nowadays lawyers and Courts refer to issues of 'residence'.

If the parents are able to agree between themselves where the children should live then so much the better. Most couples find that there is a natural solution to this problem, in that one parent may already have given up work in order to care for the children, but if there is no agreement then one of the parents will need to issue something known as a 'residence application'. This simply means filling in a form saying that you wish the Court to make an order that the child/children should reside with you, and giving brief reasons why you think this should happen. Once you have done this you will also have to file a statement that sets out your reasons in more detail than the original form.

What should be included in the statement

Both you and the other parent will be allowed to file statements saying why you each think the children should live with you. You can include any issues that are relevant to your particular family, so your statement will touch on where both parents live, the standard of accommodation, whether you work, and if so for how long, and where the children have been used to living and going to school. You would also mention if any of the children has special educational or health needs, and how you could provide for those needs if the children were to live with you. Statements in residence applications often also touch on how involved each parent has been with the children's upbringing before the separation, the standard of that care, and also whether the children have said either way where they would prefer to live.

The statements that you file will be prepared by your solicitor when he or she has had a chance to talk to you about your situation, your views on where the children should be living and why. Don't be afraid to tell your solicitor anything that you think might be relevant to your residence application. A solicitor will need to include the things that they think a judge would be interested in knowing about, and will know from experience which matters to put in and which to leave out, so don't be concerned if your solicitor has not included every tiny detail in the completed statement.

Once these statements have been filed by both you and your ex-partner there is likely to be a short preliminary hearing at Court where the judge appoints a family court adviser. FCAs (they used to be called welfare officers, so some people might still refer to them in this way) are people with a background in either social work or probation work. They are not instructed or employed by either the mother or the father but work directly for the Court, and their responsibility is to take a completely independent view of the situation and make recommendations as to what, in their view, would be in the best interests of the child.

How family court advisers compile their reports

Family court advisers have a lot of discretion as to how they go about compiling their report, but in general you can expect them to see both parents in addition to any other important family members, to visit both homes, and to see the children face to face unless they are particularly young. In some cases they will also wish to see the children in the company of each parent so that they can see for themselves how each parent interacts with the children.

Once all their enquiries are complete, the FCA will write a report that recommends where the children should live. This document is by no means binding on the Court, but it is fair to say that in the majority of cases the Court will go along with what the report recommends, unless there are very strong reasons for not doing so.

It quite often happens that at some stage during the proceedings one of the parents has a change of heart and decides not to continue with the fight over residence. This can happen for a number of different reasons, but often residence applications are started because divorces are painful, and the thought of not living with your children can be very hard to accept. Parents can also feel that they do not want to give up the chance of living with the children 'without a fight'. Often though, when looked at objectively, it can become much clearer as to where the children's best interests lie in terms of residence, and the parents can then turn their attention to sorting out issues over contact. If this is not the case, however, once all the relevant statements are filed, and the FCA has compiled his or her report, the case will be listed for a final hearing in front of a judge.

When serious allegations are being made

In some cases, once issues over either residence or contact are started, one or both parents will make serious allegations against the other. These might involve domestic violence, cruelty towards the children or sometimes even sexual abuse. An FCA reading these allegations is very rarely in a position to make up his or her own mind as to where the truth lies, especially if one person is insisting that something happened and the other denies it completely. In these situations the judge sometimes suggests there should be something called a 'perpetration hearing' before a final decision on residence can be made. This means that there will be a separate Court hearing to look at the allegations on their own and decide whether or not, in the view of the Court, they can be proved either way.

The perpetration hearing

Although having a perpetration hearing sounds like an easy solution when there are allegations flying around, in truth the hearing often ends up being one person's word against another, and it can be almost impossible for the Court to decide where the truth lies. Because of this, some judges are far less keen than others to go down the perpetration hearing route, and it would be impossible to predict in a book like this which cases will lead to a perpetration hearing and which will not. It will depend on the type of allegations that are being made, and whether a particular judge feels that a perpetration hearing would be likely to help determine what actually happened. What it is important to know is that, if there is a perpetration hearing on, say, an allegation of violence, and the judge makes a 'finding' that the violence did occur, then the FCA, whatever his or her own opinion might be, from that point on has to act as though what the judge has found is the true version of events. A finding is in some ways like a verdict would be in a criminal case, in that the judge is making a decision one way or the other as to what did or did not happen.

If that sounds a bit confusing then take this example. Alison and Tony are arguing over where the children, Lucy (6) and Victoria (3) should live. When Alison produces her statement, she says in it that Tony would never be a good father to the children because he used to smack them regularly and on one occasion hit Lucy so hard that her legs were bruised. Tony, in his statement says that this is all lies and that Alison has made these things up just to get back at him for seeing another woman.

The family court adviser does not know where the truth lies and the judge orders that there should be a perpetration hearing. At the hearing, both Alison and Tony give evidence, and the judge makes a finding that Alison is telling the truth and that her statement is the true version of events, not Tony's. The FCA must now treat the findings of the judge as though they represent the truth, whatever his or her own opinion of the evidence may be. Of course, a hearing such as this could go either way, but at least it allows the FCA to make a recommendation on a firm basis, rather than continuing to wonder whether Alison's or Tony's version of events is the right one.

Unfortunately there are cases where allegations are made, sometimes quite serious ones, and the judge comes to the view that there is not evidence to decide the matter either way. When allegations like this are left unresolved (which can be difficult for both parents), the FAC simply has to make the best recommendation he or she can in the light of the facts that are known.

Once the perpetration hearing is over, if one was needed, the case can then move on to the final hearing.

The final hearing

Once the FCA has written and submitted his report (often called the welfare report), a copy is given to both sides, and the case can proceed to Court. The hearing will be in private, so members of the public will not be allowed in. Barristers or solicitors will not be wearing wigs or gowns and the hearing itself can be either in the judge's room (called chambers) or in a courtroom, depending on the number of witnesses involved.

The FCA will sometimes give evidence first, and on other occasions will stay to the end of the hearing, listen to what the parties have to say in evidence, and then give his views at the end. Whether he goes first or last depends on the custom of that particular Court, the views of the judge, and whether the recommendation is a strong one or quite finely balanced either way. Both legal representatives will have a chance to cross-examine the FCA in either event as to the recommendations in the report and why those views were reached. The judge often talks directly to the FCA about the conclusions of the report. He will also raise any particular concerns that he may have about any issue to do with either residence or contact.

The parents' evidence

Following the FCA (if it was the FCA who went first), the parents then have a chance to give evidence, as will any witnesses they have decided to call to support their case. The Applicant (the person who applied for a residence or contact order) will go first, and will be questioned by his or her own representative (that is, barrister or solicitor). Most of the information they wish the Court to know about should already be contained within the statement, but there will almost always be at least a few matters that need further explanation. It is also useful for the judge to see how the person comes across in the courtroom. This part of the evidence is known as 'examination in chief'.

When the applicant's representative has finished, the respondent's representative will be able to ask questions of the same witness, which is often referred to as 'cross-examination'. Should any new matters arise as a result of these questions, the applicant's own barrister will be able to ask a few further questions before the evidence is finished. The judge can also ask questions directly of the witnesses at any point should he wish to; some judges are far more interventionist that others.

Once the applicant's evidence is finished, it will be the turn of the respondent to give evidence, and he will go through the same process in terms of examination in chief followed by cross-examination.

At the end of the evidence the judge will listen to final speeches (or closing submissions, in legal jargon) from both parents' solicitors or barristers, and will go on to make a decision as to where the children should live. Any hearing on residence may very well also be linked to applications on contact, and it is likely that the judge will then decide how often the parent who will not be living with the children should have contact with them.

How the judge reaches a decision on residence

One of the most common complaints we get from clients (especially those who lose in residence applications) is 'How can the judge know what is best for my children when he hasn't even met them?'. Of course this is true; a judge can only listen to what is said in Court. The welfare report is so important to the Court, and so much weight is generally attached to it, because the FCA is the person who represents the Court, meets the children and their parents and sees where they live first-hand. Whichever way a welfare report goes, whether it is in your favour or not, it is worth remembering that, while reports can always be challenged, a strong recommendation is rarely ignored by the Court. Once the report is available, it is worth taking the advice of your legal adviser as to how strong your case is, and thinking about whether you are sure you want to proceed if it has gone against you.

When making any recommendations or decisions about residence or contact, both the FCA and the judge must take into account certain things, which together are known as the 'welfare checklist'. These things include:

- The wishes and feelings of the child in the light of his or her age and understanding.

- The child's educational, physical and emotional needs.

- The likely effect on the child of any change in circumstances.

- The child's age, sex and background and any relevant characteristics.

- Any harm the child has suffered or is at risk of suffering.

- How capable the parents are of meeting the child's needs.

Both an FCA and a judge will also be very interested in how each parent would approach the issue of contact with the other should a residence order be made in their favour.

No one of these welfare checklist items is any more important than another. What is crucial is that the overall decision is, in the judge's view, in the best interests of the child when taking all the above factors into account.

The child's own view on where they want to live

There are many clients who believe, wrongly, that once a child gets to the age of ten, they will have a free decision as to which parent they should live with. This is not correct. Although the Court must take into account the wishes of a child, the amount of weight that is placed on them will vary hugely according to the individual circumstances of the case, as well as how old the child is and how clear his or her views are. I sometimes explain this to clients by saying that there is a sliding scale of weight that the Court will attach to a child's wishes: a child of three is unlikely to have much of an understanding as to where his best interest lie, whereas a child of 15 is unlikely to be ignored unless there are very strong reasons why they should not live with a particular parent.

Many clients are very upset if they feel their child's wishes have been ignored or overruled by the Court. However, the reality is that children often say to one parent what they think that person wishes to hear, and Courts are well aware of this. It is the role of the family court adviser to determine whether the child is old enough to have clear views, or whether the child has mixed feelings or an incomplete understanding of the situation. Another major factor is that the Courts are very reluctant to place the huge burden on a child of deciding which parent they would rather be with, as no child should be given such a big responsibility. So, although their views will certainly be listened to and represented in Court, the judge will use them as just one factor in deciding the best outcome for the child in the long term.

Issues of contact in residence proceedings

Once a decision on the issue of residence has been made by the judge, he will normally go on to say something on the issue of contact, so that the absent parent knows how often they will be able to see the child. The issue of contact will almost certainly have been discussed during the hearing, so the judge should be aware of all the relevant considerations by the end of the case.

Future residence applications

Clients, especially the ones who have been unsuccessful in a residence application, often ask at the end the hearings whether they will be able to make another residence application in the future.

In theory the answer is yes, although in truth the Courts are reluctant to rehear residence applications unless you are able to show a significant change in circumstances so that it is justified. One of the main aims of the Courts is to give children who have experienced marital break-up some stability, so that at least they know where they stand and that their futures are not hanging in the balance.

For this reason you would need to discuss carefully with your legal advisers whether or not applying to change residence once an order has been made is actually likely to achieve anything. In cases where one parent keeps making repeated applications for residence, and appears intent on prolonging the involvement of the Court, it is sometimes possible to apply for an order that would prevent a person making any further applications without first getting special leave of the Court.

Joint residence orders

Again, in theory, it is possible for the Courts to make a joint residence order, whereby the children's living arrangements are divided between both parents. You may also have heard of something known as 'shared custody', which refers to the same concept. For example, the children could spend three nights a week with one parent and four with the other, or spend alternate weeks between the two. I was even involved in one very unusual case where a young child stayed in one home on a permanent basis and it was the mother and father who took turns in living there with her.

However, having said that all those orders are possible, I must stress that joint residence orders are extremely unusual nowadays and are made only in exceptional circumstances. They certainly won't be made where the two parents do not get on with each other. Unless the parents can show that they have a strong ability to communicate with each other and can discuss matters that would affect the child, a Court will not even consider making an order for joint residence. The irony of it is that if two parents are still able to get on as well as this, they are unlikely to need any involvement by the Court at all. Added to that is the fact that, unless two parents live very close to each other, then a joint residence order is likely to cause problems in the child getting to school or nursery easily from two separate addresses. Perhaps the most important factor against joint residence orders, though, is that children should have a stable and secure base, and feel that they know where their home is, and living in two separate places could be confusing for them. Many parents who come expecting the Court to grant a joint residence order find this is not appropriate in their case, but that they can still enjoy an ongoing relationship with the children through weekly or fortnightly contact with them.

Contact Issues

Much of the procedure involved in sorting out contact disputes is the same as it is for residence. If you and your ex cannot agree on how much contact the absent parent should have, then one of you will have to fill in a form applying to the Court for a 'defined contact' order. The matters that the Court will consider are the same as for the residence order welfare checklist (see pages 135–6).

This just means that you will have a document that says when and how often contact between the children and the absent parent should be. You will file a statement, exactly as for the residence application, and the FCA will have to file a report on what in her view the best way forward should be.

When one parent thinks the other should not have contact with the children

Many parents are surprised, and often upset, to learn that the general rule is that wherever possible a child should have contact with both parents. There are a number of different reasons why a parent might be reluctant to allow their children to have contact with their ex, but there have to be very strong factors showing why contact is not in the best interests of a child for a Court to say that there should be no contact at all. The sorts of cases where the Court might decide to order no contact are where there has been serious domestic violence between the parents, where a child has been abused, or sometimes where the parent who has the day-to-day care of the children is so frightened or upset at the thought of contact that it would affect how well he or she was able to parent the child.

These can become quite complicated arguments, and it would take an entirely separate book to cover all the possible scenarios in a contact application. The important point to remember is that the Court will have the best interests of the child in mind, not the wishes and feelings of the parents involved.

In preparing this chapter I asked a family court adviser what advice she would give to clients caught up in a contact dispute. This is a summary of what she said:

'Parents often expect a quick solution; they want contact and they want it immediately. The difficulty with that is that sometimes the parent on the other side is not ready or able to think about contact. They forget that divorce is in some ways like a bereavement and people have to go through a number of different feelings – such as disbelief, anger and distress – before they get back into gear again and are able to think about routines and returning to normal. When someone has been through a break-up or divorce and has totally lost all trust in their ex, it is hard to then expect them to trust that person with the most precious thing in their life – their children.

'My advice is that, when this happens, you have to try and rebuild that trust. Be patient, take it step by step and don't try to rush things. Wounds don't heal overnight. You need to develop a totally new relationship with your ex from scratch or you will be stuck as an ex-husband or ex-wife forever. It is important to try to learn respect for your ex again because you cannot expect your children to respect the other parent if you find this impossible yourself. The hardest clients I have are those who simply cannot move on with their lives, and just replay the same tune over and over again.

'Try to agree things with your ex, even if this means compromising sometimes. This is almost always easier than going through the Court process. Sometimes though, where negotiation or counselling or mediation just haven't worked, the Court can kickstart the whole contact thing again and matters can end up being resolved in the long term.

'I would remind parents that children can hear a lot that is said and pick up on atmospheres. They should not be used as messengers between parents, and you should use your energy to reassure them that both parents love them, rather than just criticising the other parent all the time.

'In my experience there are very few parents who have absolutely nothing to add to a child's life and that is worth remembering. Whether you like your ex or not, the child has a right to know who both biological parents are because this helps them form their own sense of identity. A child who does not know his or her father, for instance, is likely to think that he is either something terrible, much worse than he actually is, which will affect the child's own self-esteem, or that he is a knight in shining armour who will one day come to the rescue. Neither of these fantasies will do any good in the long run. It is almost always better for a child to know her real parents for what they are, warts and all.

'At the end of the day the whole issue over contact is about what is best for the children, and not for the parents.'

There is no getting away from the fact that proceedings involving children can be extremely hard and can produce many different emotions, such as insecurity, frustration and protectiveness, but it is crucial to remember that both the parents and the Court should have at the front of their minds what will be best for the children in the long run.

If agreement can't be reached

During contact proceedings there is generally at least one hearing known as a 'directions hearing' where the Court decide what steps need to be taken (e.g. the filing of documents, or periods of contact that the FCA can observe) prior to a final hearing. These short hearings are also opportunities to put forward proposals to the other side through your legal advisers, and sometimes, if the FCA is present at Court, he might also be prepared to help you by having a discussion with your ex as to the way forward. If you feel this might help in your case, then it is always worth suggesting. Where no agreement is possible, then you have to proceed to a final hearing, which is similar to the format of a residence hearing and at the end of which the judge will make a final decision.

What a contact order might say

A judge can order as much or as little contact as he thinks is appropriate to a case. It could be as little as one hour of supervised contact a month in extreme circumstances, or (what is in fact very often decided) as much as every weekend and half the school holidays. In cases where a judge has concerns over the child's safety or his ability to cope with contact, he can order that contact be supervised. Supervision may be something that continues long-term or the condition may be lifted at a later stage. It is most common for the supervision to be by a family member or friend, although in extreme cases social services can be involved.

Indirect contact

It is also possible for a judge to order that there be indirect contact only. This means that the absent parent will be able to contact the children through letters, cards and occasional presents instead of seeing them face to face. Indirect contact orders are generally appropriate as a reintroductory step when there has not been contact for some time, where there are fears for the child's well-being for some reason, or where the mother (or father) would be too distressed by the prospect of direct contact for it to be workable or beneficial to the child.

Depending on the reasons why indirect contact was ordered, it is sometimes the case that the Court orders that there should be a review of the situation in, say, six months, to see whether or not it would be appropriate for the contact to progress to some form of direct contact. If, however, it is the Court's view that direct contact would pose a serious risk to the emotional or physical health of either parent or child, it is perfectly possible for a Court to order that contact should remain as indirect contact only.

When a parent doesn't want contact

This is a difficult situation, and one that is unlikely to resolved by legal intervention. This is, in any case, one situation where the Courts have very little power.

It is an unfortunate truth that, once a relationship breaks down, a large number of parents choose simply to walk away and lose contact with their children. I have come across a couple of cases where mothers were so desperate for their ex-husbands to have contact with the children that they applied to the Courts for a contact order forcing contact to occur. While a Court can, and often does, order that a parent *should* have contact, it does not have the power to order that a parent *must* have contact with the children. This situation can be a very tough one for a parent who is keen for the other to remain included in the lives of the children. It is an area where mediation would be likely to produce better results, if the absent parent is willing to become involved in it.

If a parent won't keep to the terms of a contact order

It is a sad fact of life that the bitterness involved in many divorces sometimes means that parents are simply not prepared to help their ex have contact with the children. Sometimes it is because a parent has genuine fears for the safety of the children but just as often, in my experience, it can simply be as a result of anger over the break-up. It is sometimes the case that, even where the issue of contact has been resolved on paper, one party still refuses to comply.

There is no easy solution to this situation. In theory, the Courts have the power to fine or even imprison a person who refuses to obey an order of the Court. In practice, however, it is very unusual for a judge to be prepared to imprison a full-time caring parent for disobeying a Court order as it would inevitably be the children who would suffer most. In the most extreme cases, a judge who feels strongly that contact should be occurring may threaten that, if the parent with whom the children live does not comply with the order, then he will order a change of residence and the children will move to live with the absent parent.

Time can be a great healer and, even after the most acrimonious of break-ups, the parent who is preventing contact may come round at some stage. It can sometimes be the case that the Court environment itself puts so much pressure on people that they behave more stubbornly than they would do otherwise. I have sometimes been surprised at how a situation that seemed totally unresolvable at one stage has moved on and, once the Court proceedings are over and tempers have cooled, the parents are able to work together and come to their own contact agreements.

However, the problem of those few parents who remain prepared to simply ignore contact orders is one for which the Courts have still not found an ideal solution.

The duration of a contact order

The idea behind contact orders is that eventually the parties will be able to move on to make their own arrangements so, while an order can specify the contact for a period of years, Courts prefer to make orders that the parties will then build upon themselves. That said, where communication is difficult it can be useful to have an order that lays down a minimum period of contact that a parent should have with the children, so that at least both children and parents know where they stand. Both parents have the right to come back to the Court at any time should they find that the order is either not working or because the family circumstances have changed, such as one parent moving away, so the current order is less viable.

CHAPTER 11

Claiming Child Support

Anyone going through a relationship breakdown will, of course, be concerned about financial security. Sorting out the finances after a divorce can be a complicated process, depending on the assets and income involved. This book cannot go into all the details of how financial settlements are reached (*Control Your Divorce,* Foulsham 2003, has a chapter devoted to the subject of finances). What I will try to do, however, is explain the system in relation to claiming money in respect of your children.

It used to be the case that the Courts had the power to determine how much maintenance a person should have to pay in respect of their children once the relationship was over. That changed with the introduction of the Child Support Agency in 1993. From that time, all claims for child maintenance (child support) were to be controlled by the agency. The Courts retained power to determine child maintenance only in very limited circumstances, or in cases where the amount had been agreed between the parties and no dispute remained.

If you are bringing up children, i.e. they are living with you and are under 16 (or 19 if in full-time education), you are entitled to claim financial support in respect of them from the other natural parent. This is the case regardless of how much you, yourself, are earning (which will obviously be to your advantage if you are a high earner). The money you receive by way of child maintenance is free of tax.

If you have managed to come to a voluntary arrangement that both parents are happy with in respect of maintenance, then there is no need to involve the CSA except if you are on benefits. If, however, you are either receiving no maintenance, or an amount that you consider to be too small, you will have to make a claim to the CSA for the correct amount to be calculated.

Your first step should be to get in contact with the CSA (see page 152) and ask for an application pack to be sent to you. In theory the pack should be with you in under two weeks, though it can sometimes take longer and you should ring again to chase it up if you have not heard anything after a fortnight has elapsed. You may have heard stories about the CSA having all sorts of complicated formulae for determining how much maintenance should be paid out. Happily, the system was changed in March 2003 to make the calculations much simpler than they used to be. Now the CSA will work out the amount of net income your ex-partner receives, and then calculate the child maintenance accordingly.

In theory, the system should be that, once your papers have been received, you are allocated a reference number and a caseworker. Make a careful note of both of these pieces of information as, in the case of difficulty, it can be extremely hard to make any progress unless you deal with the specific person who is fully aware of the details of your case. The CSA then contacts your ex to ask for details of his income. Your right to receive maintenance will start from the date that the CSA contacts the absent parent, and the amount you are owed will be calculated as from this date. Once your ex's level of net income has been calculated, the CSA will order maintenance of 15 per cent in respect of the first child, 20 per cent in respect of two children and 25 per cent in respect of three or more children.

In some cases the absent parent will pay the other parent directly, but in others the CSA takes on the responsibility of collecting the monies due and pays it directly into the bank account of the parent with care. If you have any doubts at all about your ex's willingness to pay, then this second option is certainly the one worth choosing to save you the trouble of having to chase up late payments. The CSA also has the power to obtain an Attachment of Earnings Order, which means that maintenance can be deducted directly from the absent parent's salary.

Difficulties and delays in obtaining maintenance

I should mention, though, that the CSA has reported considerable problems since transferring from their old system to the new one in 2003. Some claims are taking much longer to process than would normally be the case and for many claiming parents the whole procedure has been nothing short of a nightmare. As this is written, in early 2004, the CSA is still suffering huge computer glitches which means that there are currently many hundreds of cases that are 'stuck in the system'.

I am not defending the system, certainly not in its current format, but I do know that the CSA staff are just as frustrated as those trying to claim maintenance. The only advice I can give is to be persistent. If you find that you are experiencing problems and that your case is not being dealt with as quickly as you would hope, ask your caseworker for an explanation for the delay. If nothing still seems to be happening, make sure you chase up the enquiry until your case is dealt with. It can be absolutely maddening, and nerve-wracking, having to wait weeks or months for maintenance, especially if you are struggling financially, but remember that your entitlement starts from the time your ex is contacted so, as long as this step has taken place, arrears will accrue on the account and your ex will eventually have to pay back these as well as the ongoing maintenance amount.

If you are on reasonable terms with your ex, it might be worth asking him for an interim payment to you for the children while the CSA is sorting itself out. Any interim amount he pays will be deducted from the accruing arrears. Sadly, though, he may not be willing to pay anything until he is forced to, however patient and persistent you might be.

Useful Contacts

Community Legal Service Leaflet Line
To obtain a leaflet on family law issues for divorcing couples ring
0845 300 0343

To obtain a leaflet entitled *Parenting Plan* write to
FREEPOST
PO Box 2001
Burgess Hill
West Sussex RH15 8BR
www.lcd.gov.uk

Families Need Fathers
134 Curtain Road
London EC2A 3AR
020 7613 5060
www.fnf.org.uk

The Law Society of England and Wales
113 Chancery Lane
London WC2A 1PL
020 7242 1222
www.lawsoc.org.uk

Legal Services Commission
85 Gray's Inn Road
London WC1X 8TX
020 7759 1131
0845 608 1122 (helpline)
www.legalservices.gov.uk

London Marriage Guidance
76a New Cavendish Street
London W16 9TE
020 7580 1087
www.londonmarriageguidance.org.uk

National Association of Child Contact Centres
Minerva House
Spaniel Row
Nottingham
NG1 6EP
0870 770 3269
www.naccc.org.uk

National Council for One Parent Families
255 Kentish Town Road
London NW5 2LX
020 7428 5400 (head office)
0800 018 5026 (helpline)
www.oneparentfamilies.org.uk

National Family and Parenting Institute
430 Highgate Studios
53–79 Highgate Road
London NW5 1TL
020 7424 3460
www.nfpi.org.uk

Parentline Plus
520 Highgate Studios
53–79 Highgate Road
London NW5 1TL
020 7284 5500 (head office)
0808 800 2222 (helpline)
www.parentlineplus.org.uk

The Principal Registry of the Family Division
Family Proceedings Department
First Avenue House
42–49 High Holborn
London WC1V 6NP
020 7947 6000
www.courtservice.gov.uk

Relate
Herbert Gray College
Little Church Street
Rugby
Warwickshire CV21 3AP
01788 573241
www.relate.org.uk

Solicitors Family Law Association
PO Box 302
Orpington
Kent BR6 8QX
01689 850227
www.sfla.org.uk

Mediation

Family Mediators Association
020 7881 9400
www.familymediators.co.uk

National Family Mediation
9 Tavistock Place
London WC1H 9SN
020 7485 9066 (administration)
020 7485 8809 (information)
www.nfm.u-net.com

PDT Family Mediators
0800 028 4638

Reunite
01162 556243 (advice line)

UK College of Family Mediators
Alexander House
Telephone Avenue
Bristol
BS1 4BS
01179 047223
www.ukcfm.co.uk

You can get free copies of leaflets on many divorce-related issues such as financial matters, Court proceedings, domestic violence and mediation from your local County Court. Some of these leaflets may also contain addresses of organisations in your area worth contacting.

Quick-reference Helplines	
Child Support Agency National Enquiry Line	0845 713 3133
Children's Legal Centre	01206 873820
Gingerbread (for one-parent families)	0800 018 4318
National Association for One Parent Families	0800 018 5026
National Family Mediation	020 7485 8809 or 020 7485 9066
NSPCC	0800 800 5000
Parentline Plus	0808 800 2222
Refuge 24-hour domestic Violence Helpline	0870 599 5443
Samaritans	0845 990 9090
Victim Support	0845 303 0900
Women's Aid National Domestic Violence Helpline	0845 702 3468

Index

absent parent
  child's anger with 43,
    54–57, 73–74, 104
  child's disengagement from
    56–57, 62–63, 65
  child's dislike of 46, **84–85**
  child's relationship with
    18–19, 27, 28, 38,**41**,
    43–44, 60, 104–106
  contact with 38, 41, 98–99
  and discipline 98–99
  living arrangements 41
  reluctance for contact
    101–102, 142
  see also partners
abuse of children
  allegations in court 132–133
  and contact 84–85, 107–108,
    114
abuse of partner
  children witnessing 26–27,
    107–108
  helplines 152
  positive change to escape
    from 14
acceptance of relationship
  breakdown
  for parents 16–18, **52–53**
  for children **52–53**, 59,
    102–103
adolescence 25
adult children 16
ages of children 15–16

anger
  dealing with **54–56**, 91–92,
    95
anger, children's 60
  with absent parent 43,
    54–56, 73–74, 104
  with changed circumstances
    67–69, 99–101
  with custodial parent 43,
    47, **54–56**
arguments
  children witnessing 27–28,
    106
atmosphere, children sensing
    28–29
Attachment of Earnings
  Orders 146
attitudes to family
  breakdown 70

bed-wetting 110
behaviour, children's 15–16,
    23–25, 112–113
  during split 38–39
  parent's need to understand
    48–49
  reverting to 'younger'
    behaviour 15, 24
  taking the blame for
    breakdown 25–26
  see also emotions, children's
behaviour, parent's 31–33
  see also anger; emotions,
    parent's

blame 73–74
    children taking blame 25–26
    of one parent by adolescents
        25
breakdown of family
    children's awareness of
        21–30
    tasks for parents 31–34

CAFCASS (Children and
    Family Court Advisory and
    Support Service) 107, 114
car, access to 74
change 67–77
    and children's emotions
        13–14, 30, 67–70
    and parent's emotions 13–14
    parent's tasks 75–77
    positive aspects 14
child support 145–147
Child Support Agency (CSA)
    145–147
children
    acceptance of separation
        52–53, 59, 102–103
    adult children 16
    ages of 15–16
    anger with absent parent
        43, 54–56, 73–74, 104
    anger with custodial parent
        43, 47, 54–56
    awareness of family conflict
        21–22
    changes affecting 13, 18–19
    and court 130
    developmental stages 15,
        23–25, 36
    disengagement from absent
        parent 56–57, 62–63, 65
    dislike of absent parent 46,
        84–85
    dislike of new partners
        79–80, 82–83, 87, 105

early adolescence 25
eldest child 16
emotions after separation 61,
    65, 66, **109–111**
emotions during breakdown
    7–10, 13–14
emotions during separation
    38–40
fears of 26–27, 29–30
and grieving process 18–19,
    52–53
individual temperaments 15–16
infancy 24
listening to 60
long-term impact of
    divorce 9
maturity of 15–16
middle childhood 24–25
needs 23, **31–34**, 49–50,
    61–62
preschool 24
priority of 31–34
quizzed by parents 85
reaction to family conflict
    23–30
relationship with absent
    parent 18–19, 27, 28, 38,
    41, 43–44, 60–61,
    104–106
relationship with new
    partners 79–80, 81–88,
    89–90, 95–96
and residency decisions
    136–138
role reversal **69–70**, 75
self-centred thinking 25–26
taking blame 25–26
taking responsibility for
    breakdown 25–26
taking sides 49, 62, **65**
telling their friends 44–45
use as confidantes by one
    parent 29

views on sexuality **70–71**, 86
worry about parents 86
Christmas arrangements 72, 103
clinginess 24
co-habiting parents
and the law 9, **118–119**
communication, children's
109–110
communication, parent's 79,
83, 85, 93–94, **106**
about new partners 95–96
preparation of children
31–37, 38–39, 111–112
conduct
of parents towards each
other 13–14, 39–40
conflict
children's awareness
of 21–22
children's reactions to 23–30
contact 38, 41
children's reluctance
104–106, 107–108, 114
and discipline 98–99
and maintenance 113
see also absent parent;
custodial parent
contact and the courts 114,
138–143
contact orders 141, 142–143
directions hearings 141
indirect contact 141–142
continuity, need for 32
court proceedings
and children 130
divorce generally 117–119,
120–121, 127–129
custodial parent
child's anger with 43, 46–47,
54–56
emotions 73–75
ignoring contact orders
142–143

mismatch with child's
feelings towards absent
parent 19
support for child's
relationship with absent
parent 39, 40–41, **84,
85–86**, 104–106
custody *see* residence

decree absolute 117, 118, 121,
129
decree nisi 121, **129**
defined contact orders 138
depression 94, 110–111
and unresolved anger 54–56,
91–92
developmental stages 15,
23–25, 35–37
retreating to an earlier
stage 15, 24
directions hearings 141
discipline of children
and contact times 98–99
disengagement in relationships
22–23, 39, 56–57
children **56–57**, 62–63, 65
disinvesting in a relationship
16–18
divorce 117
attitudes towards 70
emotional aspects 7–10,
13–14, 21, 28, **31–34,
38–40**
legal aspects 9, 117, **120–121**
length of 7–9
psychological aspects 8
reasons for 22
statistics 7
domestic violence
against children 84–85,
107–108, 114, 132–133
children witnessing 26–27,
107–108

helplines 152
positive change to escape
from 14

education 37, 44, **68**, 70, **72**,
76–77
eldest child
taking on role of missing
parent 15, **69–70**
emotions, children's
after separation 61, 65, 66,
109–110
during breakdown 7–8,
13–14
during split 38–40
expressing 65–66, 109
and grieving process 18–19,
52–53
see also anger
emotions, parent's 7–8, 13–14,
21–22
after separation 61, 66,
73–74, 74–75
during breakdown 28, 31–34
during split 38–40, 42
and grieving process 16–18,
52–53
negative 92–94
see also anger
extended family
support for children 37, 40,
75

families
new 79–90
new partner's 45–46, **80–83**,
87–88
support of extended 37, 40,
54, 75, 91–92, **97–98**
family law 9
family mediation **123–126**,
151–152
FCAs (Family court Advisers)
131–136

fears, children's 29–30
of change 30
loss of contact with absent
parent 27
loss of love 26
moving house 30
feeling pain of loss 17, **53–56**
finances 67–68, 76
impact on children 37,
67–68, 72–73
friends, children's
losing 68
telling 44, 70
friends, parent's
support from 37, 54, 69–70,
75, 91–92
future plans 31–32

grandchildren
breaking news to 16
grandparents
importance of 37
grieving process 16, 42, **52–59**
and children 18–19
and parents 16–18

helplines 152
holidays 72–73
honesty needed with children
22

indirect contact 141–142
infants and conflict 24

joint residence orders 137–138

lawyers 119–120
legal aid 120, 123, 125
legal aspects of divorce 9, 117,
120–121
Legal Services Commission
123, **125**, 149
listening to children 60

loss and grieving 16, **52–59**
  and children 18–19, **52–53**
  and parents 16–18, **52–56**

maintenance 145–147
married parents
  and the law 9, **118**
maturity of children 15–16
mediation **123–126**, 151–152
middle childhood 24–25
mismatch of feelings 65
  towards absent parent 19,
    51, **52–53**, 64–65
  towards new partners 58–59
moving house 30, 68
  preparing children for 71,
    99–100
moving on 51–66
  parents 18
  tasks for parents 64–66

National Family Mediation 125
needs of children
  'lost' during separation 23,
    60, 93
  making a priority **31–34**,
    49–50, 61–62, 93
negative emotions 92–94
  see also anger
negotiation 118

pain and trauma, feeling 17,
  53–56
parenting skills
  affected by change 13–14
parents
  conduct towards each
    other 13
  deterioration of relationship
    22–23
  emotions after separation 61,
    66, 73–74
  emotions during breakdown
    7–8, 13–14, 21

emotions during split 38–40,
  42
grieving process 16–18, 42,
  52–59
honesty needed with
  children 22
individual temperaments 14
over-engaging with
  children 29
pressure on 13
protecting children 21–22
relationship after separation
  13, 39, 79
responsibility for children's
  welfare 47–48, 49–50
role changes 68–69
role reversal 69–70
tasks during breakdown
  31–34
tasks during changing
  lifestyles phase 75–77
tasks during moving on
  phase 64–66
tasks during split 48–50
tasks in new relationships
  88–90
withdrawal from children 28
working together 32–33
  see also absent parent;
    custodial parent
partners, new **57–59**, 70–71
  attitude to the children 80,
    82–83
  children's feelings about
    79–80, 81–88, 87, 89–90
  communicating to ex-
    partners about 95–96
  preparing children for
    88–90, 95–96
  step-siblings **80–81**, 88
  transient 82
  unsupportive of contact
    arrangements 102

upsetting ex-partner 81–82,
84, 87, 89
perpetration hearings 132–133
petitioner 121, 127, 129
plans for the future 31–32
preparation of children for
separation 39, 111–112
significance of 35–36
tasks for parents 31–34
preschool child and conflict 24
psychological aspects of
divorce 8

reassurance, children's need for
during breakdown 26, 27,
29, 31–34
during split 36–37, 44
reinvesting in other
relationships 18, 57–59,
70–71
relationship between child and
parents 25–26
over-engagement by one
parent 29
see also absent parent;
custodial parent
relationship between parents
after separation 13, 39, **48–49,**
92–94, 98–99, 139–140
deterioration of before
separation 22–23
disengagement from 22–23,
56–57
disinvesting in 17–18
see also communication
relationships
disengagement in **22–23,** 39,
56–57
disinvesting in 17–18
establishing new 18, 57–59,
70–71
reinvesting in 18, 57–59,
70–71

transient 82
see also partners; families
relationships, abusive 14
children witnessing 26–27
and contact 84–85
positive change to escape
from 14
relationships, new 18,
57–59, 70–71
children's feelings about
79–80, 81–88, 87, 89–90
new partners and children
80, 82–83
preparing children for
88–90, 95–96
step-siblings **80–81,** 88
tasks for parents 88–90
transient 82
upsetting ex-partners 81–82,
84, 87, 89
residence 130–138
applications 130–131
child's views 136–137
final hearings 134
joint residence orders
137–138
judge's decision 135–136
parent's evidence 134–135
statements 130–131
respondent 121, 129
roles of parents
changes in 68–69, 75
reversal of **69–70,** 75

schools
changing 37, **68, 72**
liaison with 37, 44–45, **68,**
70, 76–77, 110
separation 108
attitudes towards 70
of co-habiting couples
118–119
emotional impact of 38–40

legal aspects 117–118
of married couples 118–119
as positive experience 39
preparation of children
31–34, 35–36
sudden 40, 48
tasks for parents during 48–50
see also divorce
sexuality
children's views on 70–71
shared custody 137–138
siblings
differences between 63–64
step-siblings **80–81**, 88
social relationships and
children 37
solicitors
communicating with 131
finding 120, 151
split
emotional impact of 38–40
as positive experience 39
preparation of children
31–34, 35–36

sudden 40, 48
tasks for parents during 50
see also breakdown; divorce;
separation
stages of grieving 16–18
and children 18–19
Statement of Arrangements
127–130
step-parents 80
see also partners
step-siblings **80–81**, 88
supervised contact 141
support for parents 75
see also families; friends

taking sides 49, 62, **65**

UK College of Family
Mediators 125

welfare officers *see* FCAs
(Family Court Advisers)